DATE DUE

			PRINTED IN U.S.A.

W9-AHA-767

Easter, Passover & Festivals of Hope

Betsy Richardson

MASON CREST

Mason Crest
450 Parkway Drive, Suite D Broomall, PA 19008
www.masoncrest.com

Printed in the United States of America
First printing
9 8 7 6 5 4 3 2 1

Series ISBN: 978-1-4222-4143-1
Hardcover 978-1-4222-4146-2

Library of Congress Cataloging-in-Publication Data is available on file.

Developed and Produced by Print Matters Productions, Inc. (www.printmattersinc.com)
Cover and Interior Design by Lori S Malkin Design LLC

• CELEBRATING HOLIDAYS & FESTIVALS AROUND THE WORLD •

Carnival

Christmas & Hanukkah

Easter, Passover & Festivals of Hope

Halloween & Remembrances of the Dead

Independence Days

Lent, Yom Kippur & Days of Repentance

Marking the Religious New Year

Ramadan

Ringing in the Western & Chinese New Year

Thanksgiving & Other Festivals of the Harvest

KEY ICONS TO LOOK FOR:

 Words to understand: These words with their easy-to-understand definitions will increase the reader's understanding of the text while building vocabulary skills.

 Sidebars: This boxed material within the main text allows readers to build knowledge, gain insights, explore possibilities, and broaden their perspectives by weaving together additional information to provide realistic and holistic perspectives.

 Educational Videos: Readers can view videos by scanning our QR codes, providing them with additional educational content to supplement the text. Examples include news coverage, moments in history, speeches, iconic sports moments and much more!

 Text-dependent Questions: These questions send the reader back to the text for more careful attention to the evidence presented there.

 Research projects: Readers are pointed toward areas of further inquiry connected to each chapter. Suggestions are provided for projects that encourage deeper research and analysis.

 Series glossary of key terms: This back-of-the book glossary contains terminology used throughout this series. Words found here increase the reader's ability to read and comprehend higher-level books and articles in this field.

CONTENTS

INTRODUCTION: Celebrating Holidays & Festivals Around the World............ 6

INTRODUCTION: Easter, Passover & Festivals of Hope..................................... 8

1: Origins and Celebrations of Easter.................................... 11

2: Origins and Celebrations of Passover............................. 19

3: Origins and Celebrations of Navruz................................ 27

4: Origins and Celebrations of Holi 35

5: Celebrating in Africa... 43

6: Celebrating in Asia... 53

7: Celebrating in Europe.. 63

8: Celebrating in Latin America and the Caribbean 75

9: Celebrating in the Middle East.................................... 85

10: Celebrating in North America 91

11: Celebrating in Oceania 103

SERIES GLOSSARY.. 107

FURTHER RESOURCES 110

INDEX 111

PICTURE CREDITS 112

INTRODUCTION

Celebrating Holidays & Festivals Around the World

Holidays mark time. They occupy a space outside of ordinary events and give shape and meaning to our everyday existence. They also remind us of the passage of time as we reflect on Christmases, Passovers, or Ramadans past. Throughout human history, nations and peoples have marked their calendars with special days to celebrate, commemorate, and memorialize. We set aside times to reflect on the past and future, to rest and renew physically and spiritually, and to simply have fun.

In English we call these extraordinary moments "holidays," a contraction of the term "holy day." Sometimes holidays are truly holy days–the Sabbath, Easter, or Eid al-Fitr, for example–but they can also be nonreligious occasions that serve political purposes, address the social needs of communities and individuals, or focus on regional customs and games.

This series explores the meanings and celebrations of holidays across religions and cultures around the world. It groups the holidays into volumes according to theme (such as *Lent, Yom Kippur & Days of Repentance; Thanksgiving & Other Festivals of the Harvest; Independence Days; Easter, Passover & Festivals of Hope; Ringing in the Western & Chinese New Year; Marking the Religious New Year; Carnival; Ramadan;* and *Halloween & Remembrances of the Dead*) or by their common human experience due to their closeness on the calendar (such as *Christmas & Hanukkah*). Each volume introduces readers to the origins, history, and common practices associated with the holidays before embarking on a worldwide tour that shows the regional variations and distinctive celebrations within specific countries. The reader will learn how these holidays started, what they mean to the people who celebrate them, and how different cultures celebrate them.

▲ Christians hold an Easter vigil celebrating the Resurrection of Jesus Christ in Kanoni, Greece.

These volumes have an international focus, and thus readers will be able to learn about diversity both at home and throughout the world. We can learn a great deal about a people or nation by the holidays they celebrate. We can also learn from holidays how cultures and religions have interacted and mingled over time. We see in celebrations not just the past through tradition, but the principles and traits that people embrace and value today.

The Celebrating Holidays & Festivals Around the World series surveys this rich and varied festive terrain. Its 10 volumes show the distinct ways that people all over the world infuse ordinary life with meaning, purpose, or joy. The series cannot be all-inclusive or the last word on so vast a subject, but it offers a vital first step for those eager to learn more about the diverse, fascinating, and vibrant cultures of the world, through the festivities that give expression, order, and meaning to their lives.

INTRODUCTION

Easter, Passover & Festivals of Hope

Since early human beings first walked the Earth, spring has been a time to celebrate the renewal of the land, the source of nourishment for a community. Before agriculture, hunter-gatherer societies practiced rituals centered on the spring equinox. The spring equinox is the time in the spring when the Sun crosses the equator, and the length of the day and the night are equal. For many thousands of years of human history, in temperate climates, surviving the early spring meant survival for the year. Early spring rituals were timed with big hunts, and later with important plantings and other farming events. Ancient people could not jump into their minivans and drive to the grocery store. Their survival depended on growing food. They held rites and rituals to welcome the warmer weather and keep the corn, yam, and wheat spirits pleased. People feared that if these deities were not happy, the Sun would not shine, or there would be too much rain or, worse, there would be no rain and then plants would not grow. The ancient celebrations of spring, while often merry, were also a matter of life and death to a community. The modern springtime celebrations draw some of this ancient energy. Spring festivals sometimes overlap with New Year's celebrations as many ancient civilizations began their new year in spring, when they planted crops for the forthcoming year.

While today thousands of spring celebrations are enjoyed around the globe in the form of neo-pagan rites and environmental occasions such as Earth Day and Arbor Day, four festivals are widely observed by many cultures living in many places—from Liechtenstein to India, Argentina to Zanzibar, and everywhere in between. These four are the Hindu celebration of Holi that originated in southern Asia, the Persian new year festival Navruz, the Jewish observance of Passover (or "Pesach" in Hebrew), and the Christian Easter celebration.

Although each celebration has distinct rites and traditions, all of them share a common purpose with the ancient spring rites: They honor life and rebirth and the triumph of good over evil. As each holiday is observed, the faithful are encouraged to reflect on their actions and behavior and how they affect loved ones. At each celebration families and communities gather, dressed in holiday costumes or new clothes, to enjoy special foods and exchange small gifts. For Jews and Persians, the spring festival is also a time to clean the home and rid it of unwanted items.

▲ Piles of colored powder for sale in a market in Mysore, India, during Holi.

Origins and Celebrations of Easter

Easter is considered the most important Christian festival. Easter celebrates the central Christian belief that Jesus rose from dead three days after his Crucifixion. Christians believe Jesus was the Son of God, and died on the cross to redeem humanity from sin. In addition to its religious meaning, the Resurrection symbolizes the revival of hope and a fresh lease on life for all human beings. Christ's victory over death signifies to Christians the possible salvation of their eternal souls.

WORDS TO UNDERSTAND

Abstinence: Self-restraint or self-denial of something, such as alcohol, for a period of time.

Apostle: One chosen and trained by Jesus in the New Testament to preach the Gospel.

Bible: Collection of religious writings used in both Judaism and Christianity.

Deity: A god, goddess, or holy being.

◀ The origins of Easter come from the pagan deity, Eostre, goddess of fertility.

■ Origins of Easter

EOSTRE, THE MOTHER GODDESS

The English name for this celebration, *Easter*, takes its name from the pagan **deity** Eostre, the mother goddess of the Saxon tribes of northern Europe. Eostre was also the goddess of fertility. She was believed to be in charge of conception and birth, as well as pollination, flowering, and the ripening of fruit. After the harsh dreary winters of northern Europe, Eostre brought the warmth of spring, fertility, and abundance.

  The ancient deities in all civilizations had patron animals, and the rabbit, a symbol of fertility, is the companion animal of Eostre. In one legend, Eostre transformed a bird into a rabbit–but the rabbit kept the ability to lay eggs. Eostre's feast day occurred on the first full Moon following the spring equinox. Celebrants would combine prayers of thanks and make small offerings over fires.

▲ **Easter bunnies on display in a store window in Düsseldorf, Germany.**

REBIRTH IN THE MEDITERRANEAN

Most of the pagan societies that settled in the Mediterranean region had a major religious celebration at or following shortly after the spring equinox. A common theme of these spring religious festivals was a god whose own death and rebirth symbolized the death and regeneration of life during this time of year. There are stories of a few gods in pagan religions who were believed to have died only to be reborn.

For example, the Phrygian fertility goddess, Cybele, had a consort named Attis. (Phrygia was located within the triangle formed by the modern cities of Afyon, Eskisehir, and Ankara, the capital of modern Turkey.) Attis was believed to have been born of a virgin, and several religious historians believe that the Christian legends of death and resurrection were first associated with him. The ancient Christians, on the other hand, claimed that Satan had created counterfeit, or false, deities to preempt the debut of Jesus and to confuse humanity. Modern-day Christians, those who know of it, regard the Attis legend as merely a pagan myth. They believe the account of Jesus' death and Resurrection and do not accept the idea that it might be related to the earlier tradition.

THE ARRIVAL OF CHRISTIANITY

With the arrival of Christianity, sweeping changes took place in these ancient spring rites and ceremonies, first within cultures located along the Mediterranean and later through the lands of Europe. In order to promote Christianity as the only religion, early church leaders banned all pagan rites and ceremonies. But these rituals had been a way of life for thousands of years, and people did not easily give them up. So the Christian Church adapted, attaching Christian meanings to the old pagan rituals and festivals.

CHRISTIAN EASTER

The Crucifixion of Jesus took place on what is now called Good Friday. In the early morning of the third day after his Crucifixion, which happened to be Sunday, some women disciples of Jesus went to the cave (tomb) where his body had been laid. They learned that Jesus had been resurrected, or raised from the tomb. Grief turned into celebration following this amazing occurrence.

EASTER AND THE MOON

Even today, nature guides church planning. Christians celebrate Easter on the first Sunday after the first full Moon of spring.

Easter is not a festival confined to a single day, however. It is spread over a considerable length of time, starting with Lent, a period of spiritual preparation for Easter. In some countries, those in which Roman Catholicism is the dominant religion in particular, Easter celebrations begin with Carnival. Carnival is called Mardi Gras ("Fat Tuesday") in French-speaking countries.

■ When Easter Is Celebrated

Easter is called a "movable feast," because it is celebrated on different dates every year. The Western and Eastern Churches celebrate Easter at different times because they use different methods to schedule the holiday.

Roman Catholic and Protestant Churches of the West schedule Easter using a complicated system of rules that date to the Council of Nicea. At that meeting in 325, church leaders came up with a number of rules about how the Christian Church should work. One thing they decided was that the Church should hold a holiday to commemorate the day on which Jesus rose from the dead. Because they didn't know when this happened, they decided that Easter would be celebrated on the Sunday after the first full Moon following the spring equinox. Helpful astronomers created a chart that plotted out their estimates of the dates of full Moons for many years to come. The Church formally adopted these dates as what are called "ecclesiastical full Moons." They noted that the spring equinox fell on March 20 in 325, so they made that an official date. From then on, the rule for scheduling Easter was that Easter should fall on the first Sunday after the first ecclesiastical full Moon after March 20. The result of this complicated scheduling is that the Western Easter can fall anywhere between March 22 and April 25.

The Eastern Orthodox Easter usually comes after the Western Easter. There are several reasons for this. First, the Eastern Churches do not use the same calendar as the Western Churches. Western Churches use the Gregorian calendar, which is the calendar that is used in Canada, Europe, the United States, and most of the world. The Eastern Churches use the Julian calendar, which was the calendar in place when the rules for scheduling Easter were first set. The Julian calendar is currently 13 days ahead of the Gregorian calendar. Second, Eastern Churches use the actual first full Moon after the spring equinox to set the date of Easter. They do not use the ecclesiastical full Moons. Third, the Orthodox Easter must fall after the Jewish holiday of Passover. This is to remain faithful to the **Bible's** claim that Jesus died after Passover. With these regulations, April 3 is the earliest date on which the Eastern Churches can celebrate Easter. Sometimes the Eastern Orthodox Easter falls on the same date as it does for Western Churches. In other years it might be as many as five weeks later.

▲ A Russian woman lights a candle to celebrate Easter at a church in Moscow. Eastern Orthodox churches, which observe the ancient Julian calendar, usually celebrate Easter later than Western Churches.

THE 40 DAYS OF LENT

Lent is the period before Easter that some Christian churches observe as a time of prayer, fasting, and **abstinence**. Abstinence means giving up a pleasure (such as chocolate). Lent commences on Ash Wednesday and concludes on Holy Saturday, the day before Easter Sunday. Originally, various Christian groups established the observance as an interval ranging from a few days to several weeks. Eventually it was fixed in the eighth century at 40 days, representing the 40 days that Jesus spent fasting in the wilderness. Among Roman Catholics, Lent lasts for six-and-a-half weeks

EASTER CYCLES

The cycle of Easter dates repeats itself every 84 years in the Western Churches and every 19 years in the Eastern Churches. In other words, Easter this year will fall on the same date as it did 84 years ago and will fall 84 years from now in the Western Churches. In the Eastern Churches it will fall on the same date as it did 19 years ago and will fall 19 years from now.

before Easter, excluding Sundays. According to the Eastern Orthodox Churches, it comprises a full eight weeks since Saturdays and Sundays are both excluded.

Here's a look at some of the origins and traditions of Easter.

The last Sunday before Easter (and the first day of Holy Week) is Palm Sunday. This day commemorates the day that Jesus and his disciples entered the city of Jerusalem, where people were gathering for the Jewish festival of Passover. When Jesus arrived there was great excitement among those who believed that he was the long-awaited king of the Jews. People welcomed him by waving palm fronds and spreading palm branches as a carpet across his path.

SEDER AND THE LAMB OF GOD

The Crucifixion of Jesus occurred at the same time that the paschal lambs (for the Jewish feast of Passover) were being slaughtered. Jesus came to symbolize the sacrificed lamb of God.

The most somber of Christian holidays, Good Friday, observes the day on which Jesus was crucified by the Romans, who were threatened by his growing influence and power. As the story is told in the Gospels, the biblical accounts of Jesus' life, Jesus was arrested by Roman soldiers in the garden of Gethsemane after being betrayed by one of his disciples, Judas Iscariot. The Romans marched Jesus through the streets and presented him to the Roman governor, Pontius Pilate, who sentenced him to death. The soldiers then put a crown of thorns on Jesus' head and paraded him to the crucifixion site outside of the city. While his disciples watched, the Romans nailed Jesus to the cross, and he died. Later, Jesus' disciples took his body down from the cross and buried him in a tomb, which they closed with a heavy rock.

THE RESURRECTION

Easter is a joyous time in the Christian faith because Jesus' story does not end with his death. Early Sunday morning, Mary Magdalene and several other disciples went to his tomb and were astonished to find that the rock had been moved and the body had vanished. Two angels appeared before the women and explained that Jesus had risen from the dead. Jesus later appeared before the disciples, telling them to spread his teachings throughout the world. Belief in the Resurrection is central to the Christian faith, and Easter is the holiest of Christian holidays.

■ Celebrating Easter

Easter is celebrated by Protestants, Catholics, and Orthodox Christians throughout the world, especially in Europe, the Americas, and parts of Africa and Oceania. Most Christians attend church services Easter Sunday morning. They often enjoy a special meal with family and friends after church. On Easter morning in Europe and much of North America, children receive Easter baskets full of candy and sometimes small toys. These baskets are said to have been left by a magical figure called the Easter Bunny. The bunny also hides colored eggs for children to find. In the Western world, many non-Christians participate in Easter festivities related to the bunny rather than the church. It is believed that the hare became part of the Easter tradition first in Germany more than two centuries ago, when parents delighted children with stories about a hare that could lay eggs. The legend is connected with Eostre, who is called *Oastara* in German; the German word for Easter is "Osteon."

 TEXT-DEPENDENT QUESTIONS

1: Who was Eostre?

2: What year was the Council of Nicea?

3: How many days is Lent?

RESEARCH PROJECTS

1: Research a holiday of repentance similar to Christian Lent in another world religious tradition. Examples include the Jewish holiday of Yom Kippur or the Muslim holiday of Ramadan. Write a brief report that includes a brief overview of the holiday, how it differs from Lent, and the ways in which it is similar.

2: Research the Council of Nicea, including its historical context, the groups and individuals who attended it, and some of the issues it addressed. Write a brief report summarizing your findings, including how the council helped shape the teachings of Christianity.

Origins and Celebrations of Passover

Passover commemorates the departure of the early Jews, or Hebrews, from Egypt and the origin of a Jewish state led by Moses about 3,000 years ago. Passover signifies both the physical as well as the spiritual freedom earned by the Jews. The tale of

WORDS TO UNDERSTAND

Israelite: Someone who was part of the ancient group of Hebrew people that originally descended from Jacob, a biblical ancestor of the 12 tribes of Israel.

Observant Jews: A Jewish person who practices Judaism, the religion of the Jews. Observant Jews can be part of many kinds of Judaism, and not all observant Jews follow all of the Jewish traditions. However, observant Jews take part in the major traditions, holy days, and religious services associated with Judaism.

Plague: A disease that spreads widely and quickly through a community and often kills many people. A plague can also be a sudden eruption or emergence of something very horrible or disagreeable, such as a plague of locusts that destroys crops.

◀ A teenage boy takes part in a seder, helping to recount the story of how Moses led the Jewish people from slavery under the Egyptian pharaoh to freedom.

the Jews' mass exodus is told in the book of Exodus in the Tanakh, or Hebrew Bible (which also forms the largest part of the Christian Bible, the old Testament). Though it is mainly celebrated to remember the Exodus of the Jews from Egypt after centuries of slavery, the festival also marks the beginning of the harvest season in Israel.

■ The Origin of Passover

THE STORY OF JACOB

According to the book of Exodus, Jacob, with his 70 family members, traveled to Egypt to live a better life and escape a massive famine in Canaan (today's Palestine). Jacob's son Joseph also lived in Egypt, where he had won the favor of the pharaoh of Egypt with his wisdom and had been appointed the viceroy to govern the kingdom. Over the next 430 years the Hebrews prospered in Egypt, and their strength increased to 3 million. Their growing numbers and power became a cause of worry for the pharaoh, who thought that the Hebrews might side with his enemies to dethrone him. So he commanded that the Hebrews work as slaves, engaged in building roads and cities for him. He thought that this hardship would make the Hebrews so exhausted at the end of the day that they would have no time or energy to beget children. The **Israelites** were also confined to an area known as Goshen (the fertile land lying east of the Nile Delta and west of the Palestinian border).

When even this step did not help to slow the population growth of the Israelites, the pharaoh ordered that all Israeli male babies be killed at birth. However, the Hebrew midwives Shifra and Puah, who were appointed by the pharaoh to kill the male babies, feared the wrath of God and did not follow the pharaoh's orders.

THE STORY OF MOSES

Moses, who would become the leader of the Hebrews, was born around the time of the pharaoh's decree that all Israeli male babies be killed at birth was issued. To save her son from being murdered, Moses' mother, Jochebed, placed her child in a basket in the Nile as Moses' sister Miriam watched from a distance to see who would spot the child. The infant was ultimately found by the pharaoh's daughter. She named the child *Moses*, which means "drawn out," as he was literally drawn out of the river, and also unknowingly appointed Jochebed as his nurse. Thus, Moses' real mother was able to make certain he knew his Hebrew heritage.

Moses lived in Midian, an area situated in present-day Saudi Arabia along the eastern shores of the Red Sea, as a shepherd. One day Moses had a vision from God (referred to as the incident of the burning bush), who told him that he and his brother Aaron were the chosen ones to lead the Hebrews out of Egypt into the Promised Land, Canaan. Hesitating initially, Moses and Aaron eventually returned to Egypt.

Finally, Moses, under the guidance of God, led his people out of Egypt after God had sent a series of 10 **plagues**. These plagues had been meant to warn the pharaoh that if he did not let the Hebrews go then various afflictions would bring ruin on the Egyptians. At first the court magicians tried matching Moses and Aaron's power, but by the third plague they saw they were no match. Still, the pharaoh had not changed his mind about letting the Hebrews go. On being reminded by Moses after each plague about the imminent devastation of the Egyptians, Pharaoh would agree to let them go but would again take back his word. Finally, God had told Moses that to punish the pharaoh for enslaving the Israelites, he would send a plague to Egypt to take the firstborn son and the firstborn animal from every household. God had instructed Moses that each Israelite family should sacrifice a lamb to be eaten during a special meal. The Israelites should then mark their doors with the blood of the lamb as a signal to the angel of death to pass over their homes during the plague. From this event comes the word *Passover*, or *Pesach* in Hebrew. It was only after this 10th plague (and losing his own son) that Pharaoh finally agreed to let the Hebrews go.

Since the Hebrews left in haste, they had no time to bake their daily bread in the usual way for their trip to Canaan; therefore they baked unleavened bread called matzo. Today Jews eat matzo during Passover in memory of the Exodus.

■ Celebrating Passover

The Jewish calendar, which has been used since 3761 B.C.E., is a lunar calendar with 12 months. Each month has 29 or 30 days, making a year 354 days long. To keep the fall and spring holidays in the correct seasons, an extra month is added every 19 years. For the Jews each day begins at sundown, or dusk, and lasts until the following sundown. Holidays on the Jewish calendar drift in a range on the Gregorian calendar.

Passover begins on the night of the 15th day of the month of Nisan in the Jewish calendar (usually between the end of March and mid-April on the Gregorian calendar), and lasts for seven or eight days.

Passover is celebrated in Israel, home to almost half of the world's Jews, and in every country where Jews live, including the United States, Mexico, Canada, Argentina, and parts of Europe. As Passover is celebrated in the home, Jews prepare for the holiday by purifying their houses.

PURIFYING THE HOME

Since the Hebrews were preparing to leave Egypt in a hurry, they made special bread of flour and water that would not need time to rise. Jews remember the Exodus by eating unleavened bread, or matzo, every year during Passover. **Observant Jews** remove all *chametz* from their homes. *Chametz* includes any bread that rises in the oven, as well other foods made of grains, like wheat, barley, oats, and rye.

The removal of the *chametz* is also symbolic of the removal of self-centeredness and pride–or things that puff one up–from a person's soul. After the *chametz* has been removed, the house is often thoroughly cleaned as well. Jewish families may sort through their old or unused toys and clothes and decide which to donate to charity or to throw out as part of this thorough cleaning.

A SEDER DINNER, BOTH SACRED AND SCRUMPTIOUS

After all *chametz* has been removed and the home has been thoroughly cleaned, Jewish families observe the first night (and sometimes the second night) of Passover with a special service and meal, the seder,

Enjoy a brief presentation on the Passover seder.

during which the story of the Exodus is told. Usually the seder is led by one person, often the head of a family, such as the father or grandfather, or a special guest. Sometimes the story and the many rituals that accompany the seder are told by those at the Passover table.

Certain steps must be followed in order during the seder (in fact, the word *seder* means "order"). The steps that celebrants must follow are detailed in the Haggadah, a book filled with sacred passages, blessings, stories, songs, and psalms centering on the Exodus story. A Passover seder might last an hour or several hours, depending on how precise and thorough the leader is about following the rituals. Because Orthodox Jews strictly follow Jewish laws, they may hold a long seder, recited in Hebrew and include all the rituals. A seder for a secular (non-religious) Jewish family with young children might touch on the most important historical traditions, such as the Israelites' breaking free from slavery and leaving Egypt, but leave out numerous prayers and religious texts.

THE FOUR QUESTIONS

A central part of the observance during the seder meal is the questions that are asked by the youngest child of a family (often the youngest son) and answered by the leader of the seder meal (or sometimes by all the other people present):

THE SYMBOLIC FOODS OF THE SEDER PLATE

The foods on the traditional Passover seder plate are symbols that help tell the biblical story of the Jews' escape from slavery in Egypt. Shown here, are horseradish root, symbolizing the bitterness of bondage; lamb shank, symbolizing the blood of the lamb painted on the doors of Jewish households; salt water, symbolizing the tears of the enslaved Jews; *charoset*, a fruit, nut, and wine mixture that represents the cement between the bricks that the Jews were forced to build with; matzo, which remembers the hurried flight of the Jews that gave them no time to allow the bread to rise; and the bitter herbs, symbolizing the bitterness of slavery.

▲ The Passover seder is a Jewish ritual feast celebrating the biblical story of the Jews' escape from Egypt. Seder customs include drinking four glasses of wine, eating matzo, and partaking of symbolic foods placed on the Passover seder plate.

Why does this night differ from all other nights?

For on all other nights we eat either leavened or unleavened bread.

Why on this night only unleavened bread?

The unleavened bread is eaten because the Israelites had to flee Egypt quickly.

On all other nights we eat all kinds of herbs; why on this night only bitter herbs?

Jewish ancestors had been enslaved, which made their lives bitter.

On all other nights we need not dip our herbs even once; why on this night must we dip them twice?

The herb parsley is first dipped in salt or vinegar as a reminder of the greening that comes in the spring, and bitter herbs are then dipped in sweet sauce as a sign of hope–there was hope of freedom after the bitter years of slavery.

On all other nights we eat either sitting up or reclining; why on this night do we all recline?

Because on this night in olden times, reclining meant that you were a free man, not a slave.

These answers teach the youngest family members important historic and religious lessons.

ASHKENAZI AND SEPHARDIC JEWISH PASSOVER TRADITIONS

By geographic origins, there are two major groups of Jews: the Ashkenazi Jews and the Sephardic Jews. *Ashkenazi* is an old Hebrew word for "Germany" and originally indicated Jews who spoke Yiddish, a German dialect. Today the Ashkenazi include Jews from Germany, France, and Eastern Europe and their descendants in the Americas. *Sephardic* is derived from the old Hebrew world for "Spain." The Sephardic Jews are those who descended from Jews living in Spain and Portugal as well as northern Africa and the Middle East. Today, France is majority Sephardic since Sephardic Jews emigrated from northern Africa after the decline of the French empire in the 1950s and 1960s. Because Jews from these areas had been in countries controlled by the French, it was often relatively easy for them to adapt to French culture.

The differences between Passover celebrations among Ashkenazi and Sephardic Jews are most evident in the seder foods and traditions. For Ashkenazi Jews, in addition to *chametz,* foods classified as *kitniyot* by Ashkenazi rabbis centuries ago are also off limits on Passover. *Kitniyot* includes peanuts, beans, rice, dried fruits, and corn. For Sephardic Jews, dishes with these foods are not prohibited. Therefore, when Ashkenazi Jews make *charoset*, a fruit, nut, and wine mixture eaten during seder to represent the mortar (material that holds construction blocks together) used by the Jewish slaves in Egypt, it is almost always made with apples, walnuts, and red grape wine. On the other hand, Sephardic Jews use a wide variety of dried fruits, nuts, and often other liquids besides kosher grape wine.

During Passover, Ashkenazi Jews recite the 10 plagues that befell Egypt after the pharaoh refused to let the Israelites go. While the plagues are being described, the participants around the

◀ A boy recites from the Passover Haggadah during a seder meal in Richmond, Virginia.

seder table dip their pinky finger into their wine glasses and let the drops fall on their plates. This ritual symbolizes the Jewish belief that everyone is a child of God, even the Egyptians.

TEXT-DEPENDENT QUESTIONS

1: What is the meaning of the name *Moses*?

2: What is the name for the unleavened bread Jews eat during Passover?

3: Name one of the four questions asked during the seder meal.

RESEARCH PROJECTS

1: Research the history of the Haggadah as well as how it outlines the different components of the Passover seder. Write a report summarizing your findings, including a brief synopsis of some of the Haggadah's prayers, songs, and stories and when they are used during the seder.

2: Research the 10 plagues as described in the book of Exodus. Prepare an outline of these plagues, including ways they are described in the bible and ways that people have interpreted them throughout history.

Origins and Celebrations of Navruz

Navruz is the spring festival celebrated by people of the Zoroastrian faith, people originally from Persia (today's Iran), where Zoroastrianism was born, and in most countries located along the legendary Silk Road, an ancient trade route thousands of miles long that connects China with Asia Minor and the Mediterranean. The festival has

WORDS TO UNDERSTAND

Islam: The religion of Muslims throughout the world. This religion is based on the word of God that was revealed to the Muslim prophet Muhammad during the seventh century C.E. Islam also refers collectively to the people, culture, and countries where Muslims live.

Kurds: A group, mostly Sunni Muslims, of the same ethnicity who live in Southwest Asia in an area that includes parts of Iraq, Iran, Armenia, Syria, and Turkey. Many Kurds would like their own homeland and have been persecuted by the countries in which they live.

Monotheism: The belief in the supremacy of one god (and not many); Judaism, Islam, and Christianity are monotheist religions.

◀ For Navruz, the Iranian New Year, it is traditional to grow wheatgrass as a symbol of rebirth.

been celebrated for nearly 3,000 years. The word *Navruz* means "new day" in Farsi, the language of the Persians. Zoroastrians consider Navruz the last of the seven stages of Creation. For the people in this region, Navruz is a celebration of nature's joyful awakening after the cold winter months. It is the start of planting, cultivating, and harvesting of crops, and a time of thanks, a day when conflicts and hostilities are forgiven and forgotten.

■ Origins of Navruz

ZOROASTRIANISM

Zoroastrianism is based on the life of Zoroaster (believed to have lived around 1000 B.C.E.) who preached **monotheism** (belief in one God) in a land with a history of polytheism (the worship of many gods). Initially ridiculed for his teachings, Zoroaster eventually won over the king of Persia, and Zoroastrianism was the state religion of many Persian empires until the seventh century C.E. (the Common Era, which begins with the birth of Jesus).

Zoroastrianism is believed to be the oldest religion in the world that worships one God. Zoroaster taught that while there were other divinities, Ahura Mazda was the one uncreated God, and he made all that was good, including the other divinities. Zoroastrians believe in the central concepts of heaven and hell, the eternal struggle between good and evil, and a messiah who will save humanity.

According to ancient texts, Zoroastrians believed the world was created in seven stages. Each of these stages was historically celebrated with a feast day to honor the creations and to bring the Zoroastrian community together. However, the last and seventh creation, fire, was the most important of the celebrations, and is central to the Navruz festivities. Fire is sacred to Zoroastrians because it represents the force of life, with the Sun at its center. According to Zoroastrianism, fire purifies everything it touches: The universe was created by fire, is preserved by fire, and will be destroyed by fire. Ahura Mazda is venerated through sacred fire, which is believed to contain the prophet's presence. Because fire represents life, death, and rebirth, it is no coincidence that Navruz is celebrated during the spring equinox, the time of an ancient spring festival in pre-Zoroastrian times. Zoroastrianism is still practiced by close to 200,000 people today. Even in Iran, where it was once persecuted, it is now a protected minority.

OTHER PEOPLES ARRIVE AND CELEBRATE

In ancient times during the Navruz festival, kings would wear crowns with images of the annual solar cycle on their heads and take part in the divine ceremony that was held in the Temple of Fire. There, they would celebrate and give their subjects gifts. As Turks and other wandering peoples ventured into Central Asia and areas around old Persia, they also began to observe Navruz. Navruz traditions became deeply rooted in the lives of European and Asian farmers, and it survived the arrival of **Islam** in the area some 1,400 years ago.

View scenes of Navruz celebrations around the world.

Navruz continues to be widely celebrated in Central Asian countries, where Muslims are a majority such as Azerbaijan, Afghanistan, Iran, Uzbekistan, Tajikistan, Kazakhstan, Turkmenistan, and Kyrgyzstan. It is also celebrated among the **Kurds** in Syria, Turkey, and Iraq. Those who follow the Baha'i Faith, a religion that took root in the 19th century and originated in Iran, also celebrate

▲ Families gather to mark the spring festival of Navruz in Istanbul, Turkey. Nearly 3 million tulips are in bloom for Istanbul's Tulip Festival held during Navruz.

Navruz (though they call it Naw Rúz). During the late 20th century, many Central Asian republics made Navruz an official holiday.

■ Celebrating Navruz

WHEN NAVRUZ IS CELEBRATED

Navruz is celebrated each year on March 21 in the Northern Hemisphere, when the Sun enters the astrological sign of Aries. This date regularly corresponds with the spring equinox. In the Gregorian calendar, the spring equinox fluctuates between March 19 and 21. In some countries, the Navruz date has been changed to conform with the seasons and harvest cycles of that country. Whenever its precise start, Navruz marks the beginning of 13 days of observance of the Persian new year.

SPRING CLEANING BEFORE THE MORNING "STAR"

Navruz is traditionally a time to clean up. People clean their homes, wash draperies and rugs, adorn the house with flowers, and purchase new clothes. On Navruz, all housekeeping duties, including meal preparation and the cleaning of the house, should be complete before the morning "star" Venus appears in the sky (Venus is visible early in the morning during certain periods of the year).

Children eagerly await the arrival of Navruz because they receive gifts, money, and blessings from their elders on this day. When the day dawns, people greet one another with hugs, handshakes, and the words *Nowruze-tan Mubara* (Happy Navruz).

THIRTEEN DAYS OF OBSERVANCE

During the 13 days of Navruz, families pay respect to relatives who have died. In some places, they also go to shrines of saints and holy men and light candles in their honor.

PRAYER, SACRED FIRE, AND OFFERINGS

For religious families, Navruz begins with a morning prayer offering thanks to God. They may then light a sacred fire and burn sandalwood and incense. In some countries, a family member or religious leader reads from the Avesta (the sacred book of the Parsee, a Zoroastrian group living in western India and descended from Persian refugees) while making symbolic offerings of fruit, water, and flowers.

THE CELEBRATORY TABLE: HAFT SEEN

Zoroastrian customs require that the celebratory table, also known as Haft Seen, be displayed during Navruz. The Haft Seen table is central, as it is spread with symbolic elements, including several foods. On the Haft Seen table seven essential items are arranged. Their names begin with the letter *s* (*sin* in Persian) and commonly include:

VISITING AND PLANTING

People often visit relatives and friends in the days following Navruz; another custom is to plant seedlings of fruit trees.

Seeb (apples), for beauty
Seer (garlic), to ward off ill-health and evil *Sabzeh* (wheat sprouts), for the rebirth of nature
Sekkeh (coins), for prosperity
Serkeh (vinegar), for old age, maturity, and patience
Senjed (fruit of the lotus plant), for love
Sonbol (hyacinth), for happiness

A mirror, which reflects the past and reveals the future, and painted eggs, symbols of fertility and the sprouting of life, are also often placed on the table. These colorful spreads are tangible as well as palatable reminders of the deeper meaning of these spring traditions.

THE LAST DAY OF NAVRUZ

On the 13th day, ancient Persians believed they must be outdoors in order to avoid bad luck. In some areas, official outdoor picnics and celebrations take place in public parks and other open spaces. The 13th day is also sometimes a day to play pranks or tricks, not unlike April Fools' Day in the United States and Europe.

SETTING THE HAFT SEEN TABLE

To celebrate Navruz, Iranians set the table of Haft Seen, denoting items beginning with the letter *sin* (S). In the center of this Haft Seen is a Quran surrounded by an apple, symbolizing beauty and health; sumac berries, symbolizing the color of the sunrise; coins, representing wealth; wheat sprouts, symbolizing rebirth; a bowl with goldfish, symbolizing life; decorated eggs, symbolizing fertility; fruit of the oleaster tree, symbolizing love; and garlic, symbolizing medicine.

There are often lighted candles on the Haft Seen table, since fire is sacred to Zoroastrians. Incense is also burned to ward off evil spirits.

TEXT-DEPENDENT QUESTIONS

1: According to Zoroastrianism, how many stages did it take to create the world?

2: On what date is Navruz celebrated in the Northern Hemisphere?

3: Name an item found on a Haft Seen table.

RESEARCH PROJECTS

1: Research the history of the Silk Road and how it helped unify cultures throughout Europe and Asia. Write a brief report summarizing your findings, including items traded on the Silk Road, some of the cultures and religions it spread, and its main land and water routes.

2: Research the Avesta, the sacred book of Zoroastrianism. Find out about the history of its composition, its different texts and components, and some of its central teachings. Write a brief report summarizing your findings.

Origins and Celebrations of Holi

Among the many festivals celebrated in India, Holi is easily the most colorful and exciting, and children enthusiastically wait for its arrival. Also called the Festival of Colors, Holi is a Hindu spring festival that is celebrated for a two-day period starting on the full Moon day in the month of Phalguna, which is February or March in

WORDS TO UNDERSTAND

Diaspora: Any geographic place where a group of people from a different culture settle that is not the country of origin of these people.

Lore: The knowledge or wisdom that one has about traditions or customs that has been passed down through the generations, often through story telling.

Pyre: A large file usually built with piles of wood on which the body of someone recently deceased is cremated in a religious ceremony.

Reincarnation: The belief in some religions that after a person or animal dies, his or her soul will be reborn in another person or animal; it literally means, "to be made flesh again." Many Indian religions such as Hinduism, Sikhism, and Jainism, believe in reincarnation.

◀ Students smeared with colored powder enjoy Holi celebrations in Allahabad, India.

the Gregorian calendar. Holi marks the end of winter and the beginning of spring, as well as the flaming end of the Hindu demoness Holika. The holiday is observed with great joy throughout India and wherever Hindus live, such as Mauritius, off the coast of Africa; Nepal, Bangladesh, and Sri Lanka in South Asia; Guyana in South America; Great Britain in Europe; and the United States and Canada. Holi even offers a brief break from the strict caste system in Hindu society. Most of the year people are divided according to their ancestry and social class. But on Holi, everyone is equal.

■ Origins of Holi

THE LEGEND OF HIRANYAKASHIPU

The festival of Holi originated in the ancient Hindu legend of Hiranyakashipu. It celebrates the triumph of good over evil. According to Hindu mythology there was a demon king in India named

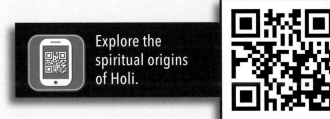

Explore the spiritual origins of Holi.

Hiranyakashipu, who wanted to avenge the death of his younger brother, also a demon, who had been slain by Vishnu (one of the trinity gods in Hinduism). In order to fight Vishnu, Hiranyakashipu sought to become the ruler of Earth, heaven, and the underworld, performing harsh penance and prayers for numerous years to please Brahma (the all-powerful creator) in order to obtain this power from him.

Finally Brahma gave the king his wish, but the demon king abused his new power, ordering everyone in his kingdom to worship him instead of Vishnu. The king's young son, Prahlada, was a devotee of Vishnu. Going against his father's wishes, Prahlada constantly prayed to Vishnu. Unable to make Prahlada change his ways, the demon king decided to kill him. The demon king asked his sister Holika (from whom the name of the festival is derived) to help him because she was supposedly impervious to fire. They planned to burn Prahlada to death and believed that she would survive while the little boy burned. So Holika sat on a burning **pyre** with her nephew Prahlada on her lap. Miraculously, Prahlada emerged unharmed by the flames and Holika, the demoness, was burned to death.

▲ Girls throw flower petals during Holi in Calcutta, India. It is traditional to throw petals of marigold, jasmine, and chrysanthemums on each other.

HOLI BECOMES POPULAR

According to Hindu belief, Krishna, a **reincarnation** of Vishnu, is believed to have popularized the colorful tradition of Holi. The origin lies in Krishna's boyhood. Krishna used to indulge in pranks—his mischievous nature is legendary—by dousing the village girls with colors and water. Initially the girls were upset, but they were so fond of the boy that his popularity overcame their anger. Other boys joined in and made it a popular sport in that village. With time the tradition stretched to all regions of India, and, having survived through the ages, it has become a community festival for everyone.

▲ Celebratory bonfires, like this one in Jaipur, India, are common sights during Holi.

■ Celebrating Holi

WHEN HOLI IS CELEBRATED

Like other Hindu festivals, Holi customs and traditions can differ significantly depending on the region. The length of the festival can also vary. In some places in northern India, Holi can last up to a week. In the state of Manipur in northeast India, it is a six-day festival. But in most places it is a two-day festival, starting on the eve of the bonfires and continuing the next day with the Festival of Colors. It always begins some time between the end of the February and the end of March.

ON THE EVE OF HOLI A FIRE IS LIT

On the eve of Holi, also called Choti Holi ("Small Holi"), celebrants light bonfires on street corners to send away the cold dark winter nights and usher in spring. Hindus perform music, dances, and

FORTUNE-TELLING WITH ROASTED SEEDS

In some Hindu Holi celebrations, barley seeds are roasted in the fire and then "read" in order to see whether the coming harvest will be a good one. In other locations, it is the directions taken by the Holi bonfire flames that help predict the future. The fire cinders are also said to have healing powers, and Hindus sometimes take them from the dying fire at the end of the night to rekindle their own house fires.

▲ Boys throw colored water during Holi celebrations in India. Holi, the Hindu festival of color, heralds the arrival of spring.

tell traditional stories around the fires to celebrate Prahlada's miraculous survival and the death of Holika, his wicked aunt. People take cinders from this bonfire to rekindle their own house fires. The bonfires are generally made from cowdung cakes, logs of wood, honey, ghee (semifluid clarified butter), and harvest offerings.

FESTIVAL OF COLORS

In a tradition especially loved by children, Hindus gather during Holi to cover one another with colored powder, battle with squirt guns, and toss water balloons. On the streets of India during Holi, it is impossible to avoid a multicolored downpour.

Hindu **lore** offers at least three stories about the origins of the colored powder. According to one story, Krishna (a reincarnation of Vishnu) is believed to have popularized the colorful tradition of Holi when he would douse the village girls with colors and water. Another story holds that when Krishna was young, he often complained to his mother, Yashoda, about his companion Radha's light complexion and his own dark skin. Yashoda told him to put color on Radha's face and watch how the color of her skin changed.

Perhaps the most dramatic story associated with the origin of the powder on Holi involves the popular monkey god, Hanuman. One day, it is said, Hanuman swallowed the Sun, leaving the people in utter darkness. The other gods, pitying the dejected people, suggested they rub color on each other to cheer themselves up. This they did, mixing the color with water and squirting each other gleefully. When Hanuman saw what they were doing, he could not help himself and let out a huge laugh, accidentally spitting out the Sun again and returning light and color to the world. All over India and the **diaspora**, these are a few of many stories told on this day to explain the remarkable and joyous Holi powders.

TEXT-DEPENDENT QUESTIONS

1: What is another name for Holi?

2: What is Choti Holi, and how do Hindus celebrate it?

3: Describe one of the stories of the origins of the colored powder used during Holi celebrations.

RESEARCH PROJECTS

1: Research one of the major Hindu deities, such as Shiva, Vishnu, Shakti, Ganesha, and Surya. Find out information about their appearance, what elements, energies, or subjects they are associated with, stories about them in Hindu literature, and other facts. Write a brief "biography" of your chosen deity summarizing what you've learned.

2: Research the holiday of Maha Shivaratri, which also takes place during the Hindu month of Phalguna. Write a brief report including facts about its history, what it celebrates, and ways in which Hindus observe the day.

▲ Teenage Indian girls dance in celebration of Holi in their village temple complex.

Celebrating in Africa

Various Christian European customs and religious beliefs found their way to the vast continent of Africa during the colonial era, especially sub-Saharan Africa. Likewise, much of northern Africa is Muslim due to its long-term trade arrangement with Middle Eastern neighbors to the north. Brought by Muslim traders and Christian colonizers and missionaries, Christianity and Islam retain a strong foothold in Africa. But long before these two monotheistic faiths were introduced, Africans believed in a supreme power that created the world. This supreme power has several different names and forms as

WORDS TO UNDERSTAND

Ancestor worship: Rites and rituals used by cultures to honor the connection between the living and the dead, especially those of one's family.

Archipelago: A chain or large group of islands in an ocean.

Liturgy: The kind of worship or service that is set forth by a religion. A liturgy can also refer to the specific way a Christian church (often Eastern Churches) celebrates Communion.

◄ An Ethiopian Christian pilgrim carries a cross on Good Friday to commemorate the path Jesus took when he carried his cross on the day of his crucifixion.

 A woman prepares for a baptism during an Easter Sunday ceremony in Johannesburg, South Africa.

varied as the thousands of cultures of Africa. In most African faiths, God is said to have created the Earth and then left the day-to-day workings to lesser gods, ancestral spirits, elders, rainmakers, and other mediators. Important tribal members who have recently died may also serve as spirits to whom the community gives offerings and prays—for a good harvest, more rain, or crop returns. The dead are also considered better able to speak to the spirits, helping to keep them pleased. Many Africans, even those who are Muslim and Christian, believe the dead must be taken care of by the living and that there is a connection between the dead and the fertility of the land. To honor this connection, festivals are celebrated throughout Africa during planting and harvest seasons.

Spring celebrations in Africa are festive and sometimes intense, often with a mix of drumming, dancing, athletic contests, and ancient rites. Easter is celebrated in many parts of Africa. Like Christians in the rest of the world, African families go to church on Easter morning, decked out in new clothes and hats, ready to celebrate the renewal and rebirth of their faith, their God, and the land. In some countries of Africa, Easter festivities are blended with local rites and customs, such as traditional drumming and dancing. Also, in some villages, non-Christians are invited to Easter feasts in the homes of their Christian friends and relatives. While the Christian Easter is widely celebrated, parts of Africa also celebrate Navruz, and other spring rites. Other blended or distinctive springtime celebrations include those for Hili, Tafsit, and Sham El Nessim.

■ Camel Races during Tafsit in Algeria

During the colonial era, from 1830 to 1954, traders from Algeria, Libya, Niger, and northern Mali would meet in the Algerian town of Tamanrasset for a great festival. The main attraction was the

▲ Camel races are the main attraction at the Algerian Festival of Spring.

camel race, with each tribe putting forth its best camel rider. The festival continues, though it has been modernized and renamed Tafsit, or the Festival of Spring. It takes place in April and its slogan is "friendship discovered" because it traditionally brought together traders from many places to celebrate the spring. Algerians love this festival, which enables people to gather and share various musical and cultural traditions. The camel race is still the main attraction.

■ Easter in Côte d'Ivoire

For Christians in the western country of Côte d'Ivoire (Ivory Coast), Easter is a rare joyful time in a country that has endured a devastating civil war in recent years. Christians make up 20 to 30 percent of the more than 18 million living in Côte d'Ivoire. These Christians follow many Holy Week traditions. On Maundy Thursday they hold services in which devout Christians wash the feet of new believers in imitation of Jesus and his disciples. On Good Friday, some evangelical Christians go door to door in non-Christian communities to evangelize, or try to convert people to Christianity. Holy Saturday is a happy and spiritual time for Christians of Côte d'Ivoire, who stay up all night, dancing, singing, and praying until the dawn of Easter morning.

On Easter Sunday churches are decorated with ribbons to celebrate Jesus' Resurrection. Devout Christians attend church with friends and family. Singing and dancing are part of the celebrations, as people swing joyfully to the rhythm of drumbeats. After church, Christians share a special Easter dinner that consists of roasted or boiled rice served with meat.

■ Coptic Easter and Sham El Nessim in Egypt

Copts, as Egyptian Christians are known, celebrate Easter with great fervor. Copts identify strongly with Jesus' Crucifixion and Resurrection, as they themselves have been persecuted over the centuries for their beliefs. Coptic Easter, which occurs in March or April according to the Coptic solar calendar, is the most important feast for Coptic Christians. They spend the day with family and friends, often picnicking at sites such as the Urman Gardens in Cairo, Egypt's capital. In the 55 fast days leading up to Easter, and more than 150 other fast days during the year, Coptic Christians follow a vegan diet, excluding all meat products or foods that come from animals, even milk and cheese. Copts believe that the Bible instructs them to eat vegan food during many fast days because it was the food eaten when God first created the world, before humans and animals began to reproduce and to live sinful lives.

On the first Monday after Coptic Easter, Muslims and Christians throughout Egypt celebrate Sham El Nessim, which means "sniffing the breeze." For more than 4,500 years this holiday has commemorated the start of the harvest season. In ancient times, salted fish, lettuce, and green onions were offered to the gods to ensure a good harvest. In modern-day Egypt, people enjoy picnics featuring traditional foods, including a variety of salted fish known as *fiseekh*. Just as in other spring celebrations, eggs are dyed in bright colors and symbolize the renewal of life.

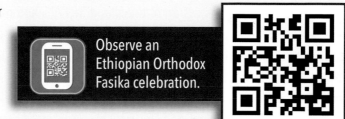

Observe an Ethiopian Orthodox Fasika celebration.

■ Celebrate with Flames and Food in Ethiopia

Christianity spread throughout the eastern African country of Ethiopia in the fourth century, when two Christian brothers became stranded there and eventually converted the Ethiopian royalty. The Ethiopian Orthodox Church, associated with the Coptic Church of Egypt, is among the oldest Christian denominations in the world. Until 1975 the Ethiopian Orthodox Church was the state Church of Ethiopia. Though the Church's influence has declined in recent years, facing competition from Islam and Protestantism, 35 to 40 percent of Ethiopia's people still identify themselves as Orthodox Christian.

On the eve of Ethiopian Easter, called Fasika, Orthodox Christians attend midnight Easter services at which candles are lit. Easter concludes a 55-day fast during which Christians have eaten only one vegetarian meal a day.

After church on Easter, Christians break the fast by eating meat with pancakes made of *teff*, a grass flour, and by drinking honey wine or beer. Easter, like Christmas, is a time to gather with family and exchange gifts.

■ Holi Celebrations in Mauritius

In Mauritius, a small island in the Indian Ocean off of South Africa, Holi is a major spring holiday. This is largely due to Mauritius's history. Mauritius was an uninhabited island before the arrival of the Europeans. The Dutch settled the island in 1598 and named it Mauritius after Prince Maurice of Nassau. France took possession of the island in 1715 and governed it until 1810, when British forces seized control. During British rule, in 1835, slavery was abolished and indentured laborers were brought from India. An entire society, from priests to business people to craftsmen and farmers, arrived at Mauritius from India. Over the next 200 years, these people practiced their Hindu faith on the isolated island, largely undisturbed by outside influence. Since 1948, when property qualifications were abolished and the franchise was made universal, the Indian community has dominated the legislature.

Today, Hindus, who now make up 48 percent of the population, celebrate Holi in Mauritius (now a republic in the British Commonwealth) as they would in India—with bonfires and colorful

▲ Children pray during an Easter ceremony outside a church in Sudan.

water fights. There is singing, dancing, and lots of music. It is a time for festive rejoicing. In the evenings, people visit each other's homes and exchange greetings.

Easter in South Africa

Christianity has a long history in South Africa. The country was colonized in the 17th century by the Dutch, who were seeking diamonds and gold and brought their Christian faith with them. Though Europeans no longer rule South Africa, Christianity has remained there. Denominations include the Zion Christian, which makes up 11 percent of the population, as well as Pentecostal, Catholic, Methodist, Dutch Reformed, and Anglican.

Together, Christian faiths make up close to 80 percent of the population. Of these faiths, the Zion Christian Church (known as the ZCC) has the most dramatic and elaborate Easter festivities. For several days, millions of church members travel to celebrate Easter in Zion City, home to the original founder of the Church, Engenas Lekganyane (ca. 1880–1948). Today the ZCC, founded and still led by black Africans, is one of the largest independent Christian Churches in the country.

The ZCC members believe in the power of their religion to heal. This can lead to troubles with traditional African healers, called *sangomas*. Yet despite occasional problems, the ZCC respects traditional African religious ways of life, especially the role of **ancestor worship**, the power of the ancestors to intervene on behalf of humans. South Africans can participate in ancestor worship and also be members of the ZCC. The members of the ZCC are proud that their religion was founded and is led by Africans and is an entirely black church that responds to black African needs. Unlike some Christian churches in African countries colonized by Europe, the ZCC's **liturgy**—or the form of worship that the Church allows—includes traditional South African singing and dancing.

Mwaka Kogwa Means Navruz in Zanzibar

A unique Navruz celebration called Mwaka Kogwa takes place over a four-day period in Zanzibar, an island which is part of several islands off the east coast of Africa. Centuries ago Persians from southern Persia (now Iran) first arrived in Zanzibar and the other east African islands grouped with it. They came in order to escape hardship and famine and were the first group to settle Zanzibar in large numbers. Arabs in later years used the Zanzibar islands as a convenient trading base for their ivory and spices because the islands were small and easy to defend. Today, Zanzibar, part of the nation of Tanzania, is 99 percent Muslim and many old Persian traditions are still followed.

The Mwaka Kogwa festival is celebrated all over Zanzibar, including the larger islands of Unguja and Pemba, as well as smaller islands in the Zanzibar **archipelago**. The biggest and most famous celebration takes place in Makunduchi, in southeastern Unguja. Like Navruz celebrations elsewhere, during Mwaka Kogwa people believe that God and spirits help them purify the past year and welcome the new one. However, this New Year's celebration has taken on many traditions and customs of its own over the generations, including unique traditions that involve symbolic combat and a burning hut.

The highlight of Mwaka Kogwa is the ritual battle between two brothers chosen from northern Makunduchi and two brothers from southern Makunduchi who fight each other in the center of town on the first morning of the new year. Often former presidents or other dignitaries are guests of honor for this opening tradition.

During the mock combat, the brothers from the two parts of town hit each other with banana tree branches, because the branches split on contact. The combat follows rules passed down through the generations, until one side surrenders. Sometimes other townsmen enter the fight, and any boy who can keep up with the men, too, giving every male an opportunity to let out his grievances. The people of Zanzibar believe that this fight allows a fresh start in the new year and to let go of hard feelings. While the men fight, the women, dressed in their best attire, parade around the field and sing songs in Kikae, a local Swahili dialect. The songs, which are about life and love, gently tease the men. Nowadays, the men tease back with songs of their own.

With the fight almost over, villagers build a pyramid-shaped hut out of coconut thatch and everyone's focus soon shifts to this hut. With the crowd gathered round, a local shaman (a spiritual guide and healer believed to be able to divine the future) enters the structure that is then set on fire by the crowd. With the hut fully ablaze, the shaman rushes out unharmed, and dives into a bush. The crowd then douses the hut's flames and everyone celebrates. It is believed that because the shaman is not hurt by the flames, no one will be hurt in the coming year if a house should catch fire.

When the mock fighting and hut burning is over, the celebrants go home and prepare for a huge feast. The cows, already butchered in preparation, will now be cooked. The villagers come back together for the feast, which is held outside. Everyone is welcome, family and strangers alike. In fact, people believe that a villager must share the meal with a guest in order to be happy on this day. Finally, people gather in their most colorful clothes to dance *ngomas*, the traditional dances accompanied by drums. The dancing often goes on all night.

TEXT-DEPENDENT QUESTIONS

1: What is Tafsit and where is it celebrated?

2: Who are the Copts?

3: Where is Zanzibar?

RESEARCH PROJECTS

1: Research an African harvest festival from a country of your choosing. Write a brief report outlining where and when the festival takes place, how it is celebrated, its historical significance, and other details.

2: Research facts and information about Coptic Christians. How are their beliefs similar to those of other Christian denominations and how are they different? Write a brief report summarizing your findings.

Celebrating in Asia

Asia is the world's largest continent in size and holds almost three-fifths of the world's population. Many cultures and religions **intermingle** in this vast region. For instance, India, a country almost 81 percent Hindu, also has a significant Muslim population (about 14 percent), while Kazakhstan is more evenly divided between Muslims (47 percent) and Orthodox Christians (44 percent). Persian and Muslim influences are strong throughout Central Asia. In some areas, such as Turkmenistan and Azerbaijan, Muslims today make up more than 90 percent of the population, many of Persian ancestry.

From Easter in Macau, to Navruz in Kazakhstan, and Holi in Nepal, Asian spring festivals are a whirlwind of color, cuisine, and culture. In Hong Kong, Japan, Nepal, or Kyrgyzstan in the spring, the sweet and mellow aroma of incense hangs in the air,

WORDS TO UNDERSTAND

Bazaar: A large marketplace or shopping area, usually outdoors.

Intermingle: To blend or mix.

Sovereignty: The right of a people, region, or a country to govern themselves without intervention or interference from outside political and cultural influences.

◄ People celebrate Holi in Madras, India, dousing each other with colored powder and water.

▲ Artists perform in costume during Navruz celebrations in Kazakhstan.

EXCITING NAVRUZ TRADITIONS

During ancient times in Central Asia, Navruz was observed in agricultural areas with bazaars, horse racing, festivals, and cockfights. The Uzbeks (people from Uzbekistan and neighboring areas) passionately adhere to their traditional dish *sumalyak*, a molasses-flavored cream of wheat prepared with flour and sprouted wheat grains. Sprouted grain is the symbol of life, abundance, and health.

having been lit by families to purify their surroundings and send away evil spirits from the home or from beloved ancestors' graves. Dust fills the air too, from intense spring cleaning rituals before Navruz festivities in Central Asia.

The flames burn brightly around the spring equinox in India and Nepal, as Hindus joyously cast old objects into the Holika flames on the eve of Holi. Flames purify the Earth to ward off evil during a multitude of spring celebrations around Asia. And while eggs are often closely associated with Christian Easter and the Navruz Haft Seen table as symbols of rebirth and fertility, they are also tied to biblical stories involving Jesus' mother, Mary, in the Orthodox Armenian Easter.

Throughout Asia, spring is a time for friendship and the possibility of new love, as well as for a bit of healthy flirting among young adults. Food and gifts–either toys or treats to eat–play an important role in many Asian spring festivals.

Watch scenes of Narvuz in Azerbaijan.

In March, all over Central Asia houses and barns are cleaned to prepare for the Persian New Year and spring celebration of Navruz. When Islam first spread across Central Asia, Navruz was banned by some Muslim rulers because it was not originally a part of Islam. But people continued to celebrate, and eventually the ban was lifted. Navruz is widely celebrated in Iran (formerly Persia) and other countries with centuries-old Persian influence, such as Afghanistan, Azerbaijan, Kazakhstan, Kyrgystan, Tajikistan, Turkmenistan, and Uzbekistan.

As in other parts of the world where people of Persian descent have settled, Navruz in Asia begins with a thorough cleaning of homes and washing of draperies, tablecloths, and other household items. People also prepare by setting the Haft Seen table, lighting incense and candles in their homes to ward off bad luck and spirits, visiting the graves of their loved ones, eating special foods, and exchanging small gifts.

■ Navruz, a Revered Imam, and Red Flowers in Afghanistan

In Afghanistan, Navruz symbolizes happiness, peace, friendship, and reconciliation around the country. Afghans thoroughly clean their homes before Navruz to show their willingness to entertain the spirits of their ancestors. Some Afghans believe that Ajuzak, a threatening old woman, roams the countryside on Navruz. Rain on New Year's means that Ajuzak is washing her hair, a sign that the harvest of the coming year will be a rich one.

In the city of Muzar-e Sharif ("Tomb of the Saint") in northern Afghanistan during Navruz, a flag is raised at the shrine of Hazrat Ali. The city was founded in the 12th century after a local religious leader dreamed that Ali, son-in-law of the Prophet Muhammad, was buried there. Ali is known as Hazrat Ali in Afghanistan. Thousands of people visit the shrine hoping to touch the staff in order to be healed by its powers or to receive Ali's blessing.

During Navruz the Red Flower Festival is also held at Mazar-e-Sharif to welcome and celebrate the spring season. On the first day of spring, the meadows of Afghanistan are covered with wild red tulips (which give the festival its name), as well as poppies, daisies, and violets. Against the backdrop of the gorgeous mountains that divide the Kabul Valley, everyone gathers to enjoy picnics and kite-flying contests.

On the night of Navruz, Afghans often eat *sabzi chalau*, a spinach and rice dish that is sometimes served with lamb or chicken, and *samanak,* a sweet dish made especially for the new year that requires elaborate preparation. Two to three weeks before Navruz, wheat is planted in small pots. From this wheat young women make this sweet pudding that is meant to celebrate a good harvest and the beginning of the new year.

▲ A group of dancers perform during the Hindu festival of Holi, or festival of colors, in northern India.

Holi Traditions in Hindu India

Depicting the rich variety of Holi celebrations in India is like trying to describe the view through a turning kaleidoscope–there are fascinating variations of scenes that all involve magnificent colors in endless entrancing patterns. In the northeastern region of Bengal Hindus place a statue of the deity Krishna, in his form as a child-god, in a cradle in front of the Holi bonfire. In Sri Dhama Mayapur, a town in West Bengal north of Calcutta, they also parade a statue of the saint of Bengal, known as Mahaprabhu Chaitanya, down the city's streets. In some parts of northern India, effigies (figures or carvings) of Holika are thrown into the bonfires. Newly harvested stalks are given as offerings to Agni, a fire God. In India Holi provides a great spring release as young men and women douse each other with color, or, in one tradition, engage in mock battles between the sexes.

In northern India, an exuberant tradition takes place every year in the small town of Barsana. Barsana is the home of Radha, the teenage love of Krishna. Not far away is the town of Nandgaon, Krishna's hometown. One week before Holi starts in the rest of India, the young men from Nandgaon converge on Barsana and try to raise a flag over the Hindu temple there. As the men run through town in large groups, the women of Barsana clobber them with sticks, trying to capture them and prevent them from reaching the temple. The men wear foam pads to protect their bodies, but they are not allowed to strike back. The women punish the men they capture by dressing them in saris, the traditional women's dress of India. The "prisoners" are also dolled up with women's makeup and commanded to dance.

The following day, Barsana's men take revenge by going en masse to Krishna's town of Nandagaon. Now the women of this town get to flog the Barsana men. It is all in good fun, as the tourists who attend can clearly see. The festival concludes on the third day in a special temple nearby where numerous celebrations take place, including playing Holi (the act of decorating oneself or others in color) with pink and white powder.

Sugar and Spice for Navruz in Kazakhstan

In Kazakhstan, people welcome the spring by asking forgiveness for their sins, paying off old debts, and renewing friendships. Seven is a significant number during Navruz, and so everyone visits seven houses and invites seven guests to their homes. During this festival people play games and sports matches. The Kazakhs are known for their ability to ride horses. One sport, called *kazakhsha-kyres*, requires men to wrestle one another while each contestant is mounted on a horse. The first one to pull

▲ **Women perform during Navruz celebrations.**

the other off his horse wins. In another sport, *kokpar*, teams of men on horseback compete to capture a slaughtered goat's body. Navruz is a joyous time in Kazakhstan, marked by parties, dance, drama, and music festivals. Festive Navruz dishes include sugared wheat porridge and cinnamon-spiced veal.

■ The White Month Brings Spring in Mongolia

In Mongolia, the lunar New Year is called Tsagaan Tsar. Its exact date depends on the cycles of the Moon and can fall anytime between the end of January and early March. Tsagaan Tsar means "the white month," the color white standing for purity, happiness, wealth, and well-being. Tsagaan Tsar is the start of the milk-producing and breeding period of cattle, and people hope that spring will bring an abundance of dairy products. Families start planning for the holidays a month in advance by cooking lots of food, purchasing gifts, and cleaning out their homes and sheds. Women also make clothing for the family to wear on Tsagaan Tsar. During the Tsagaan Tsar festivities, celebrants throw red dough representing their enemies (or the enemies of Buddhism) into huge bonfires.

The New Year's Eve of Tsagaan Tsar is called Bituun and is the time when family and friends eat the last dinner of the old year. This meal often includes sheep's head or lamb's meat. Each family prepares the most lavish meal possible and friends and family exchange food dishes. On this night in some regions, it is common to visit the family of married daughters. The following morning, everyone wakes up early to greet the rising Sun, and then family members exchange greetings and gifts, usually something modest such as socks, or a drink. Mongolians then celebrate the New Year for three days or more, eating foods such as dumplings called *buuz* and sheep's back and tail. They drink fermented mare's milk, vodka, or *tsagaalga,* which is a milk drink with rice.

It is said that at Bituun a local goddess called Baldanlham is riding her horse during this period and that she will come by each house three times. Every family sets out three pieces of ice for her horse to drink. On Tsagaan Tsar, as on other Mongolian holidays, people sing songs and play games. In ancient times and still today, the men of the family take their children to an *ovoo,* an arrangement of stones on a hilltop, with trays of food and other offerings to show their gratitude to nature.

THE FLOUR FORECAST

Mongolians believe that if there is more meat in the *buuz* (dumplings) than flour, the family will have enough clothes in the coming year. If there is more flour, a family will have enough food. If there is the same amount of meat and flour, everything will be right for the year.

■ Holi Lasts a Whole Week in Nepal

Hindus make up more than 80 percent of Nepal's population. In Nepal the weeklong Holi celebration is called Rung Kelna, or "playing with color." The night before Holi begins festival-goers light huge bonfires and burn images of Holika to cleanse the area of evil spirits and to symbolize Holika's death.

The next day the *chir* (or *chit*) pole—a greased pole decorated with colorful flags—is set up at Durbar Square in Kathmandu to mark the beginning of the festival. People wear old clothes because old and young alike throw water balloons and colored powder at one another throughout the day. In other parts of Nepal the festivities revolve around a 25-foot-tall umbrella. At its base people light sticks of incense and leave flowers and red powder. Then they toss water-filled balloons out of upper windows, a clever way of drenching someone else without risking retaliation.

The last day of the festival is a wild one indeed. Young men cover themselves with red powder and arm themselves with water pistols, water balloons, and more colored powder as they wander the streets of the city, making themselves targets for the multitudes.

■ Easter in the Philippines

Due to the influence of Catholic Spain in colonial times, the Philippines is more than 80 percent Roman Catholic. In the Philippines people attend midnight prayer services for Easter and celebrate Jesus' Resurrection by lighting candles. Christians parade through the streets pulling *carrozas* (carts) carrying elaborate full-sized figures from the Easter story, including Mary, Jesus, Judas, and Pontius Pilate, among others. These processions are also popular in Spain and in Latin America, which was colonized by Spain even before the Philippines.

■ Navruz Marriage Traditions in Turkey

Turkey's Navruz customs are quite exceptional. In many parts of the country on the night of Navruz, young men who want to get married eat half a *tuzlu gyllyk*, a special pastry made from salted wheat dough. After eating, they do not drink water so that they go to bed thirsty, believing that they will marry the woman who offers them water in their dreams. On the following day they place the remaining half of the *tuzlu gyllyk* on the roof or chimney of their homes. If a crow takes the dough and flies away with it to another rooftop to eat it, then the man will marry the daughter who lives in that house. But if the crow grabs the pastry and flies away without stopping, the man will marry a woman from a faraway land.

In the Kars region of northeast Turkey on the evening of Navruz, young unmarried men and women gather at one house and send a child to fetch a bucket of water. After the child returns, the men toss colored threads into the bucket, and the women throw in pins. It is believed that those whose threads and pins become intertwined will marry each other.

■ Celebrating the Rainy Spring Season in Southeastern Turkmenistan

In some areas of Turkmenistan, Navruz celebrations are directly tied to the rebirth of the land and to farming. Turkmen, who make up 75 percent of the population, observe two distinct

Navruz periods in the southeast of the country, one related to breeding cattle that takes place in February, and a longer one related to agriculture, Ypek Navruzi, in March.

The Persian-speaking population of southern Turkmenistan celebrates the new year's holiday as Navruzi Eid. During the holiday, people attend open-air fairs, where they build swings, cook various dishes, and paint eggs. On Navruz they boil a meat soup of wheat barley and dress it with yellow raisins and other dried fruits. During Navruz Eid, celebrants visit their friends and relatives, bringing food as a gift. Other Turkmen people celebrate with music, plays, traditional games, sports, beauty contests, poetry nights, and other activities.

 TEXT-DEPENDENT QUESTIONS

1: In what Afghan city is the shrine of Hazrat Ali?

2: What is *kulich*?

3: What do people burn to purify their homes during Navruz in Kyrgyzstan?

RESEARCH PROJECTS

1: Select one of the countries profiled in this chapter and research facts about its history, geography, form of government, art and culture, and other details. Write a brief profile of the country based on your findings.

2: Research music and songs affiliated with Easter, Passover, Navruz, Holi, or other festivals of hope. Find out information about instruments used, lyrical content, popular performers, and other associated facts. Write a brief synopsis of your findings.

Celebrating in Europe

Easter is the spring festival most widely celebrated throughout Europe, and here, perhaps more than anywhere else in the world, it is clear that Easter is both a holy day that celebrates Jesus' Resurrection and a spring celebration with ancient pagan roots.

All over Europe (especially in the north), as well as areas of European influence such as the Caribbean, people play egg-rolling and other egg-related games that take place on the day after Easter to commemorate the rolling away of the rock from the mouth of the cave where Jesus was buried. In England, Germany, and Ireland children roll colorfully died, hardboiled Easter eggs down green, grassy slopes. The child whose unbroken egg reaches the end of the slope first is declared the winner. In another game,

WORDS TO UNDERSTAND

Ascension Day: After Easter, the day of Jesus' Resurrection, comes Ascension Day, when Christians believe that Jesus rose from Earth into heaven.

Mead: A type of liquor made with honey.

Monk: A holy man who removes himself from society to live in a religious community. There, he dedicates himself to a life or period of life of prayer, seclusion, and meditation.

◄ Colorful Easter eggs are on display for the Pysanky festival in Kiev, Ukraine.

two opponents battle by knocking hard-boiled eggs against each other. The winner receives the loser's broken egg and sometimes another small gift from the host of the event. All across Europe people light candles as part of their Easter celebration.

As in many parts of the Christian world, the Easter hare brings European children baskets full of small toys and candy on Easter morning. The hare also takes charge of hiding the Easter eggs around the gardens, yards, and parks of Europe for children to find. Like the egg itself, hares and rabbits are ancient signs of fertility.

In some parts of eastern Europe people celebrate Easter Monday through a raucous tradition with ancient roots. It is in part a flirting ritual (like some Holi traditions) where men gently whip women or pour water on them to ward off evil spirits.

While the majority of the European population is Christian and Easter is the spring festival most widely celebrated throughout Europe, Jewish people also live all over Europe and celebrate the spring observance of Passover. There are more than 1.5 million Jewish people living in Europe, with more than 1 million in the European Union countries. The largest Jewish populations live in France (more than 600,000) and the United Kingdom (275,000). Outside of the European Union, Russia has the largest Jewish population, at close to 265,000 people.

In addition to Easter and Passover, many European countries also celebrate Labor Day (or May Day), as a spring festival in early May. While Labor Day is a holiday to honor the rights of workers throughout the world, many parts of Europe combine this observance with ancient rites and customs to welcome the warm weather and celebrate the fertility of the Earth. Labor Day festivities that celebrate spring are especially common in northern Europe, where it is often just beginning to warm up in early May. Other festive aspects of spring observances include festivals such as Martenitsa, the Bulgarian holiday involving the wearing of little dolls for good fortune.

◼ Lighting Candles in Andorra

In Andorra people light candles during a vigil and at midnight services the night before Easter. Then on Easter they light a special candle to signal Jesus' Resurrection. That candle is lit every day for the next 40 days until **Ascension Day**–the day that marks Jesus' Ascension to Heaven–when it is finally put out.

◼ Martenitsi Dolls Help Usher in the Spring in Bulgaria

Bulgarians celebrate a unique spring festival called Martenitsa on the first day of March, which they consider the beginning of spring. On this day, Bulgarians wear small, woven red-and-white

▲ Bulgarian *martenitsi* dolls represent happiness and prosperity. Bulgarians traditionally wear these dolls on their wrists and clothes until they see a stork, which is thought to be a sign of spring.

woolen dolls, either on their wrists or fastened to their clothes. Called *martenitsi*, the dolls represent happiness and prosperity. The red and white colors on the dolls represent the purity of the white snow that will soon be gone and the onset of spring, with its sunny days. Bulgarians are supposed to wear these dolls until they see a stork, which is thought to be the sign of spring. In some areas, people tie the *martenitsi* on a fruit tree to transfer their good luck and prosperity to the fruit-bearing tree. On Easter, like other Europeans who use candles in their Easter observance, Bulgarian Christians hurry into the streets after midnight mass with burning candles in their hands.

■ Gingerbread Lambs and Spirited Rituals in the Czech Republic

In the Czech Republic, families bake gingerbread in the shape of a lamb for Easter dinner. Young girls also decorate Easter eggs, which they give to boys on Easter Monday when the boys come to the girls' homes to sing hymns. A nationwide contest is held to select the most beautifully decorated Easter eggs. Family and friends exchange red eggs to wish one another happiness, good health, and prosperity.

In the Czech Republic Easter Monday is also known as the day of *pomlazka* (whip). Since pagan times men have used their *pomlazkas* to ward off evil spirits by whipping girls and livestock on the legs. Today young boys gently whip girls on their legs and douse them with water. While whipping them, the boys sing an Easter song asking the girls to give them Easter eggs. As a reward for protecting her against evil, a girl hands an Easter egg to a boy and ties a ribbon on his *pomlazka*. Today, girls also give ribbons, bread, and brandy as signs of gratitude.

Easter Poetry Riddles in Denmark

In Denmark children send *gækkebrev*–anonymous letters written in poetic form–to their family members on Easter. The letter is often a beautiful paper cutout with words written in the middle. Recipients have to guess the names of the *gækkebrevs'* writers. If the recipients do not guess correctly within a period of time, they have to give the senders decorated chocolate Easter eggs. The Easter celebrations continue through Easter Monday, a public holiday in Denmark.

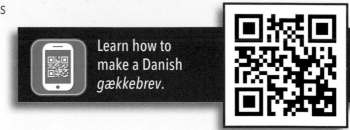

Learn how to make a Danish *gækkebrev*.

Vappu in Finland

In Finland, Labor Day is celebrated with Vappu, an ancient spring festival. It is a time for workers to conduct parades and rallies and for Finns to herald the arrival of spring, though it may still be snowing. Street carnivals, feasting, and drinking **mead** (liquor made with honey) are highlights of the day.

▲ **A Good Friday service held outside the Notre Dame Cathedral in Paris.**

■ Easter in France

In France families dress in their best clothes to attend church on Easter. Afterward they share large meals and children receive specially decorated chocolate Easter eggs from their parents and grandparents. Feasting and exchanging greetings and Easter eggs continue through Easter Monday the next day.

■ Another Meaning for Eggs in Hungary

Early Sunday morning, children awake to find small gifts of candy and toys beside their beds. A traditional breakfast of Easter eggs, ham with horseradish, braided cake bread, and hot chocolate follows. Horseradish is eaten with the Easter breakfast ham because the overpowering odor of horseradish is traditionally thought to ward off evil. According to legend, babies who eat horseradish will not get colic, a stomach pain that leads to uncontrollable crying.

On Easter Monday, traditionally young men would pour buckets of water over young women's heads to ward off evil and protect them from harm. The women rewarded the men with kisses and eggs painted red, the color of passion. Today, instead of pouring water, they spray perfume and exchange painted and chocolate eggs.

■ Easter Granny in Lithuania

Earlier on Sunday, after the Easter church service, the woman of the house shells a blessed Easter egg and, after breaking it carefully, hands a piece to each family member to ensure that there will always be love and peace in the family. Children hunt for colored eggs, which are not hidden by the Easter Bunny, but rather the Easter Granny, known as Velyku Senele. Children are told that Velyku Senele travels across Lithuania in a cart led by Easter bunnies and stops at homes to place decorated eggs and sweets either in the yard or in special Easter baskets. Only those children who have behaved well are rewarded with sweets and brightly colored eggs, while those who have been bad receive a single white egg.

■ An Easter Bonfire in the Netherlands

On Easter, devout Dutch Catholics attend Mass in their local churches. A beautiful Easter wreath hangs on every door, and homes are decorated with spring flowers. In the rural areas, almost every village celebrates Easter by lighting a bonfire on a hill or a high piece of land. Each village tries to outdo the others with the biggest bonfire, for which villagers collect wood long in advance.

■ The Emmaus Festival in Poland

On Holy Saturday Polish families take baskets of food to be blessed. These baskets contain *kielbasa* sausage, eggs, Polish bread called *babka*, salt, pepper, and often a little sculpture of a lamb (usually made out of sugar) with a flag showing the cross, symbolizing Jesus. These ingredients are used to prepare the Easter meal on Sunday. In addition, ham, white sausage, smoked bacon, cheesecake, and lamb-shaped cake, are very popular.

On Monday in Kraków, Catholics celebrate the ancient festival of Emmaus, commemorating the risen Christ's encounter with two of his disciples on the way to the town of Emmaus. On this day in ancient times young men fought each other with sticks, trying to show off their strength to young women. Many men also courted women by gently hitting them with willow twigs.

More commonly celebrated on Easter Monday is a Polish tradition called Smigus Dyngus, or "Wet Monday." On this day boys douse girls with water using squirt guns and buckets. The more a girl is drenched, the more likely it is that she will get married. Girls get their revenge the following day, when they can spray the boys as much as they would like. Easter Monday is a time for

◀ **A priest blesses parishioners' food baskets outside a Warsaw church on Easter Saturday in Poland.**

religious parades as well. During these parades celebrants carry holy pictures throughout the city, accompanied by bands and church choirs. Children are given sweets and toys on this day.

Jews Celebrate Passover Openly in Russia

When Russia was part of the Soviet Union, Russian Jews had to celebrate Passover in secret, for fear they would be punished or even jailed. Under Soviet rule, and especially between the end of World War II in 1945 and the end of the Soviet Union in 1992, all religion in Russia was suppressed.

Check out some Passover preparations in Russia.

Until recently, some Russian Jews had never celebrated Passover and were unfamiliar with its rituals and traditions. Today, and since the fall of the Soviet Union, new synagogues are being constructed in Russia. In these synagogues and other community centers, Jewish leaders are helping elderly and middle-aged Russian Jews to better understand their history and traditions through lectures, movies, meetings, and plays. Local schools are also being brought into the fold and Jewish children are learning about the Passover traditions that have not been openly practiced since their great grandparents were alive. Many Russian Jewish synagogues and organizations are also holding community Passovers to bring Russian Jews together.

Sprinkling Day in Slovakia

In Slovakia the ancient tradition of symbolically pouring water on young women to ward off evil spirits is referred to as Sprinkling Day, and on Easter Monday young men and boys are free to pour water on single and married women alike. The girl or woman gives a colored egg to the boy or man to thank him for driving away the evil spirits.

Effigies and Easter Parades in Spain

On Easter Sunday some of the faithful in Spain make an effigy, or rough model, of Judas (or some unpopular politician) out of straw and burn it. Judas is the disciple who betrayed Jesus to the Romans. Spanish Christians also perform dramatic reenactments of other important Easter stories.

▲ A set of effigy sculptures for the parade at the Fallas Festival in Valencia, Spain, to mark the beginning of spring. As the finale of the festival, sculptures and effigies made of wood and other flammable materials are burned to welcome the coming of spring.

GOT EGGS?

It is not always a rabbit that brings or hides Easter eggs. In Switzerland it is the cuckoo, while in the historical northeast German area known as Westphalia, it is the fox.

In one, a child dressed as an angel is lowered from the sky by a rope to remove the veil covering the Virgin Mary's face, reenacting the angel's appearance before Mary after her son's Resurrection. Spanish families then gather to celebrate Jesus' Resurrection and sing traditional Easter hymns. They also march in colorful parades (*cofradia*) with magnificent floats. Easter Monday is a day for egg-decorating contests, music, and feasting—especially on chocolate buns and cakes.

■ Eiertütschen in Switzerland

On Easter in Switzerland entire families gather to celebrate the Resurrection of Jesus. Children receive specially decorated Easter eggs made of chocolate from their parents and grandparents.

In the mountain valleys of Switzerland, where winter lasts for more than six months, Easter not only signifies the Resurrection but also the reawakening of nature. This rebirth of life is celebrated by sharing wine and blessed bread and donating gifts to the poor–a tradition, called Osterspende, that has been followed since the 16th century. In Switzerland dining and exchanging greetings and Easter eggs continue on the next day, Easter Monday. The custom of egg cracking, known as Eiertütschen locally, is extremely popular. In the towns of Frümsen, Oberriet, St. Gallen, and Effingen, in the canton of Aargau, the custom of egg throwing takes place every Easter Sunday or Monday. The participants in this game throw the brightly colored eggs at spectators, who retaliate by eating them right away. This festive day ends with music and dance.

BALD EGGS ARE OUT

In Ukraine as in so many other places, Easter eggs are given as gifts. One Ukrainian superstition says that girls should never give their boyfriends a *pysanky* that has no design on the top and bottom of the egg. If the egg is bald, it is thought that the boyfriend will soon lose his hair.

■ Easter Egg Traditions in the Ukraine

Perhaps the most beautiful and carefully designed Easter eggs in the world can be found in the Ukraine. In a process called *pysanky*, which means to design or to write, Ukrainians use a stylus filled with melted wax to draw intricate pat-terns on the eggs. Then when the egg is dipped into dye, the wax resists the dye. This process is repeated many times for each egg. By the end the egg is multicolored and beautiful.

In the past, all *pysanky* dyes came from natural materials such as boiled onion skins or buckwheat husks, black hollyhocks or birch leaves. Since these are natural dyes, the colors are muted and earthy, rather than bright or pastel like the colors often seen on North American Easter eggs. The colors and designs also have meanings associated with them. For example, a design of pine needles symbolizes health, endurance, and youth, while a ladder stands for prayer and prosperity. Green means spring, hope, and new growth. White represents purity, innocence, and birth. Today, *pysanky* artists have fun experimenting with new technology and new dyes. They can buy electric styluses that maintain the wax at the perfect temperature and use colors that were unavailable previously.

▲ Ukrainian Easter eggs decorated by *pysanky*, a traditional process that dates back more than 2,000 years.

Originally, these dyed eggs were part of pagan rituals. The *pysanky* designs reflected nature: the Sun, plants, animals, and weather. After the introduction of Christianity, *pysanky* became associated with Christ's Resurrection in addition to the return of spring. Christian symbols were added to the repertoire, and new materials were introduced. For example, some artists dip the eggs in a light coating of wax and then press beads into the wax before it cools. Thus, each *pysanky* is individual, reflecting the artistic preferences of each artist, and the special meanings that he or she wishes to express.

■ Hot Cross Buns in the United Kingdom

Hot cross buns are characteristic of Easter in England. Consisting of sweet bread made with yeast and decorated with an icing cross, these buns are believed to have originated in pagan times. The buns became associated with the Roman Catholic Church in the 14th century when **monks** started giving them to the poor on Good Friday.

When Henry VIII broke with the Roman Catholic Church, he wanted to ban the tasty buns, too, but the English people would not give them up. In the 16th century, Queen Elizabeth I passed a law that allowed their sale, but only on Easter and Christmas. Hot cross buns are still traditionally eaten on Easter Eve wherever Britons live.

◀ Hot cross buns arranged on the dinner table for Easter in London.

TEXT-DEPENDENT QUESTIONS

1: Where is Martenista celebrated?

2: What is Vappu?

3: Name three foods popular in Poland during Easter.

RESEARCH PROJECTS

1: Research more about the *gækkebrev* tradition in Denmark, including methods of constructing one (the Educational Video in this chapter might help). Create, write, and send a *gækkebrev* to a person of your choosing.

2: Research some of the popular colors, motifs, and patterns of Ukrainian *pysanky*. Write a brief outline summarizing some of your favorite *pysanky* themes and symbols as well as the meanings behind them.

Celebrating in Latin America and the Caribbean

B ecause it is located in the Southern Hemisphere, September, October, and November are spring months in Latin America. Still the months of March and April bring celebrations of many faiths. Processions and **passion plays** proclaim the Christian Holy Week all over Central and South America, while English-influenced Easter

WORDS TO UNDERSTAND

Gefilte fish: A food often served in shaped cakes or balls and often eaten during the Jewish celebration of Passover. This dish contains chopped fish with cracker crumbs, eggs, and spices.

Indentured servants: An immigrant to the Americas or Australia between the 17th and 19th centuries who agreed to work for an employer for several years in exchange for his or her trip to the new country and for food and shelter.

Passion play: The reenactment, or retelling, of a central religious experience or event for a religious people. For example, the suffering and persecution of Jesus Christ that begins with the Last Supper and ends with his Crucifixion is often reenacted in passion plays before Easter.

◀ Churchgoers carry a statue of Jesus during an early morning Easter procession in Paraty, Brazil.

celebrations take place alongside Hindu Holi festivities in parts of the Caribbean. In March or April every year in Argentina, a large and long-established Jewish community celebrates Passover in both the Buenos Aires capital, and on cattle ranches in the countryside. In addition, a modern version of an ancient celebration takes place during the spring equinox, which brings together local Mayans and tourists to remember and re-create the traditions of the ancient groups of Mesoamerica.

A huge majority of Latin America has practiced Roman Catholicism since Spain first conquered and colonized most of this diverse continent more than 500 years ago. But Spain was not the only European nation that sought Latin America's vast mineral, agricultural, and human resources so many years ago. The English also colonized parts of the Caribbean and South America, as did the Portuguese in Brazil. This influence can still be seen today. In the Bahamas, for example, hot cross buns and egg-rolling competitions are still popular.

The British also brought **indentured servants** from India to do the hard labor in post-slavery Latin America. Not surprisingly, Hindu Indians brought along their vibrant Holi tradition, which has colored the springs of Guyana, Suriname, and Trinidad and Tobago, ever since. In some parts of Latin America, Holi celebrations embrace all cultures in a particular region, and non-Hindus are more than happy to share in the good times.

Today approximately 70 to 80 percent of Latin Americans identify themselves as Catholic, and Latin America is the home of almost half of the world's Catholic population—around half a billion people. While this is a huge number and percentage, in recent years many Protestant Christian groups have gained membership throughout Latin America. Chile and Brazil have growing Protestant communities, and in Guatemala, Protestants make up a full 20 percent of the population. A growing branch of Protestantism in Latin America in recent years has been the Pentecostal Church, which proclaims the Bible as the literal word of God and that a direct relationship with him through acceptance of Jesus is the only way to enter heaven. Pentecostals share much in common with other evangelical faiths, including the belief that serving God requires converting others to Christianity.

SPECIAL EASTER FOODS IN THE CARIBBEAN

Jamaicans feast on an Easter treat called *bulla*, a round cake eaten with avocado. Other traditional Jamaican Easter foods include plantain tarts, banana bread, bread pudding, and sweet potato pudding. Martiniquais of Martinique (a French Island in the Caribbean) prepare a special Easter dish of crab mixed with rice called *matoutou*.

In many parts of Latin America Easter is a sacred holiday that does not involve dyeing eggs or eating candy. But in other places, candy is a focus, and chocolate eggs make

Experience Holy Week festivities in Latin America.

their appearance in stores many weeks ahead. On Easter, people exchange chocolate bunnies and large chocolate eggs, sometimes filled with hard candy or bon bons, and wrapped extravagantly in colored foils. Wealthy Brazilians might spend more than $100 on a chocolate egg for the special people in their lives.

Throughout the region Holy Week, or Santa Semana, is celebrated in full, marked by public performances and passion plays. In the lead-up to Easter, businesses and schools are closed all over Latin America.

■ Passover in Argentina

The largest population of Jews in Latin America lives in the city of Buenos Aires. In fact, Argentina is home to more than 200,000 Jews, which is the seventh-largest Jewish population in the world. The earliest Jewish settlers to Argentina were farmers who lived in agricultural colonies. Over the years, many Argentine Jews moved from farming to cattle ranching, a huge industry in a country that is famous for its beef around the world.

Despite living on a continent that is overwhelmingly Catholic, Argentine Jews have held fast to Passover traditions. In Argentina just as in every place where Jews live, Passover means cleaning the house of *chametz*, coming together as a family for the seder meal, reading the Haggadah and teaching the youngest family members about the Jewish Exodus from Egypt, and the ritual of the Passover meal.

Passover also means wonderful foods such as **gefilte fish** with horseradish, matzo ball soup, and roasted chicken. In Argentina pre-made Passover foods such as matzo ball mixes and unleavened bread have only recently been widely available in stores. As a result, Jewish families have traditionally prepared the holiday meal together at home from scratch.

■ Easter in the Bahamas

Easter in the Bahamas is a joyous time, in part influenced by British customs dating back to colonial times. Worship services begin before dawn, marking the end of the Easter Vigil that began on Holy Saturday. There are parades and feasts to mark this special day, and young girls and women

EGGS AND BREAD

Egg-rolling competitions are popular among children in the Bahamas, as they are on other Caribbean islands with British influence. Caribbean Christians also prepare hot cross buns, the European bread that symbolizes the death and Resurrection of Jesus.

wear colorful Easter bonnets decorated with ribbons, stencil drawings, paints, flowers, dried flowers, and other decorative materials. The day after Easter is known as Easter Monday and the first day of Bright Week. People enjoy feasts and parades and indulge in traditional activities: Catholics and Anglicans douse each other with the perfumed holy water that they received on Easter for use at home. Egg-rolling competitions are also popular for children.

■ Holi in the Caribbean

During the late 1800s, the British, who had colonized parts of the Caribbean and northern South America, brought indentured servants from India to harvest sugarcane and other crops, replacing the African slaves who had been freed. Today, Guyana in South America is about 35 percent Hindu and Suriname and the islands of Trinidad and Tobago are both more than 20 percent Hindu. Though they may never have set foot in India, these Caribbean Hindus know how to throw a raucous and all-embracing Holi celebration.

As in many parts of the world, Holi lasts for two days in the Caribbean. On the night of the full Moon before Holi, Hindus of Guyana, Suriname, and Trinidad and Tobago gather around a huge bonfire just as their fellow believers do in other parts of the world.

In Guyana, Hindus also invite non-Hindu Guyanese to join in the festivities and initiate them by covering them with colored powder. Music is an integral part of the celebrations. Guyana's Hindus dance to traditional Indian music played on a wide variety of musical instruments, such as the *dholak* (drum) and *jhaals* (little finger cymbals). In Suriname, Hindus wish each other "Holi Mubarak" ("Happy Holi") and throw colored powder, water, and water balloons on each other. They distribute sweets among their neighbors on this day and sing traditional songs. As in Guyana, non-Hindus also join in the celebrations. In Trinidad and Tobago, Holi includes various sports events and contests such as flag-grabbing and eating *roti* (a flat unleavened Indian bread).

The joy of Holi is that it seems to dissolve old disputes and animosities between community members, young and old alike, if only for one day. In these small Caribbean countries, people of all faiths live together in a relatively small space. It is not uncommon to see many non-Hindus

▲ Surinamese Hindus stand around the bonfire that marks the first day of the Holi spring festival. Bonfires that signify the burning of the demoness Holika are attended by many of Suriname's large Hindu population and are followed by the spring festival of colors.

participating in Holi celebrations, be they Christian or Muslim. In fact, in Guyana, some Muslim and Hindu religious observances are public holidays–including the Muslim Eid al-Adha, Eid al-Fitr, and Mouloud, and the Hindu celebrations of Diwali and Holi– although both are minority religions.

Proximity between people of different faiths and the national recognition of important holidays provide opportunities to learn about and share cultures and traditions with people of other groups and faiths. While relations are not always harmonious, the people of the Caribbean take pride in their festivals. There is even a saying among Hindus during Holi: "Do not be angry, it is Holi."

SENDING PRAYERS UP IN THE SKY

In Grenada, Trinidad and Tobago, and Guyana, Easter Monday brings remarkable kite-flying competitions, with prizes awarded for the best kites. For some, the kite flying symbolizes the Resurrection of Jesus. In Guyana, kite flyers often tie wishes or prayers to their kites. As the kites fly higher, their strings are cut in the hope that the kites will carry their messages to God.

■ Easter in Grenada

Easter in Grenada is marked by prayer services held early in the morning. During the Easter weekend the old and young alike take part in flying kites, which come in many shapes, sizes, and colors. In addition, the Easter holiday signals the beginning of the season when Grenadians picnic at the beaches, watching regattas (boat races). In Grenada these races are collectively called the Grenada Round-the-Island Easter Regatta and include short races as well as the well-known race around the islands.

■ Vivid Easter Processions in Guatemala

On Easter in Guatemala worship services begin quite early in the morning. Guatemalans celebrate the day by wearing the traditional Mayan attire and participating in processions through the streets carrying statues of Jesus. In certain regions of Guatemala, such as in the city of Antigua, Easter celebrations are known for their elaborate and beautiful processions that are attended by thousands of locals as well as tourists from all over the world. Along cobblestone streets, intricately designed carpets made of colored sawdust and other natural materials are laid down. Later a solemn procession of actors playing Roman centurions, or soldiers, marches over the carpets, carrying a statue of Jesus hanging on the cross. The delicate sawdust carpets are kicked up as the procession passes over them and are destroyed, not to be seen again until the next Easter.

■ A Mayan Spring Observance in Mexico

Since ancient times the Maya have celebrated the spring equinox by gathering at the ancient city of Chichén Itzá, constructed more than 2,500 years ago. Created with materials from the surrounding jungle in the southeastern Mexican region of the Yucatán, and without the aid of the wheel or metal tools, Chichén Itzá is an incredible assembly of buildings and pyramids that demonstrates the sophistication of the ancient Mayan society.

The Maya are known for their remarkable achievements in mathematics (they invented the concept of zero well before Western civilizations) and astronomy. They developed a sophisticated calendar that accurately tracks the changing seasons. In fact, the pyramid of El Castillo (the castle) at Chichén Itzá was built to be aligned with the Sun and work as a massive sundial to accurately show the spring equinox and the autumn solstice. Since the Maya planned their lives and planting times (especially the planting and harvesting of corn) around the seasons, this gigantic sundial was essential to their survival.

In ancient times on the morning of the spring equinox, the Maya would gather to watch the Sun form triangles on the top of one side of El Castillo. These triangles would appear in greater numbers throughout the day and then work their way down the pyramid like a gigantic sunlit snake. The snake was known to the Maya as Kukulkan, or feathered serpent, and El Castillo also

▲ The massive 75-foot high stone pyramid, El Castillo, at the ancient city of Chichén Itzá, Mexico. The staircase railings of El Castillo were carved with feathered serpents in such a way that the snakes seem to travel down the steps to the plaza with the movement of the Sun.

goes by the name Kukulkan. At the base of the pyramid, the Maya carved heads of the feathered serpent and one of them is illuminated by the end of the snake's descent on the spring equinox.

For the Maya, the descent of the snake in the form of sunlit triangles symbolized the delivery of prosperity from the heavens to the people. It told them when to start planting the crops in the spring. In the fall, the sun snake started at the base of El Castillo and slithered back up the pyramid, signifying the autumn equinox, or time to harvest the crops.

The Mayan cities were abandoned for hundreds of years even before the arrival of the Spaniards, and many were destroyed after the Spanish colonized Latin America. Nevertheless, in recent years the ancient spring equinox observance has been revived, bringing thousands—including the ancestors of the ancient Mayans and tourists alike—to Chichén Itzá and El Castillo to watch the snake's descent.

■ The Firing of the Judases on Easter Sunday in Mexico

The Firing of the Judases in San Miguel de Allende–also home to a devout passion play–is an Easter tradition that has grown so popular with tourists that it is now sponsored by hotels and other businesses. At 1:00 P.M., after church on Easter, in a central garden in the city, huge papier-mâché replicas of unpopular people–former presidents, politicians, and, of course, Judas Iscariot–hang from ropes that are extended from trees to buildings around the plaza. The oversized puppets have firecrackers tied around their waists.

At the designated hour, all the fireworks are set off in a series of enormous explosions, after which paper arms, legs, torsos, and hands float to the ground. Although often only the head remains dangling from the rope, the event is not as morbid, as it might sound. It is festive and fun, especially for the kids, who grab the blown off papier-mâché body parts and duel with other armed children. Sometimes the lonely heads are taken down and sold to tourists.

▲ A congregation prays during Easter services in the Metropolitan Cathedral in Mexico City, Mexico.

Easter Festivities in Uruguay

Uruguayans enjoy a weeklong holiday throughout Holy Week. In parts of the country the week is also celebrated as La Semana Criolla, or "Rodeo Week." Gauchos (Uruguayan cowboys) entertain the crowds with their stunts and horseback-riding skills. On Easter day itself, Uruguayans visit their friends and family members and exchange greetings.

TEXT-DEPENDENT QUESTIONS

1: Where is the largest Jewish population found in Latin America?

2: Name an achievement of the Maya.

3: How is Holy Week celebrated in Uruguay?

RESEARCH PROJECTS

1: Research key facts about the history of Jewish life in Buenos Aires, such as when Jewish settlement began, historical challenges, and contributions to the local culture. Write a brief report covering what you found. Be sure to include information about notable Jewish neighborhoods such as the Once district.

2: Research another pre-Columbian civilization in Mexico besides the Maya, such as the Olmec or Aztec. Write a brief report outlining the civilization's history, contributions to world culture, religious rituals, and other important information.

Celebrating in the Middle East

Though most countries in the Middle East are predominantly Muslim, the biggest spring festivals in this part of the world are Navruz, celebrated by Persians in Iran; and Passover celebrated by the Jews of Israel. Although many Persian Muslims celebrate Navruz, it is not originally a Muslim holiday. Around the time when their neighbors are celebrating Navruz, Jews are observing Passover. In Israel, the official Jewish state established after World War II, Jews make up close to 77 percent of the population.

■ Navruz in Iran

On the Wednesday evening before Navruz begins, many Iranians observe a custom that has been compared to Halloween. On this night, bonfires are lit in the streets and people

WORDS TO UNDERSTAND

Conquest: When one group or nation takes another over by force.
Kibbutz: A communal farm in Israel.
Shahnameh: The national epic poem of the Persian world.

◀ An Iraqi Kurdish woman dances during Navruz celebrations in northern Iraq. Navruz, an ancient Persian festival, is celebrated on the first day of spring in countries including Iraq, Turkey, Afghanistan, and Iran. The festival is mainly a Kurdish event in Iraq and Turkey.

▲ Children enjoy sweets, like sweet rice cookies, for Navruz.

jump over them as a way of celebrating the end of the old year and any bad luck associated with it. Because it is believed that spirits of dead ancestors come out on this night, children dress up, covering their heads as if in mourning. The children go to their neighbors' houses, banging on pots with spoons in the hope of getting sweets and dried fruit.

Perhaps the most important part of the New Year ritual is setting the Haft Seen with seven items. In addition, today in Iran many Haft Seen tables include an Iranian book called **Shahnameh** (The epic of kings) rather than the Quran, the holy book of Muslims. The *Shahnameh* is the national epic poem of the Persian world written by Persian poet Ferdowsi around 1000 C.E. It relates the real and mythic past of Iran from the time of the creation of the world up until the Islamic **conquest** of Iran in the seventh century. Some Iranians feel that the *Shahnameh* is more suitable on the Haft Seen because it is a reflection of Persian values and identity.

On the night before the new year, most Iranians prepare and cook a special dish of fried fish and herbed rice. Often a baked egg dish that contains an assortment of fresh herbs called *koukou sabzi* is also served. The next day, the traditional food will be rice and noodles.

In modern Iran, Navruz lasts for 13 days. The exact second that Navruz begins is called "Saal Tahvil." After the Saal Tahvil, people hug and kiss and exchange happy new year greetings and presents. Traditional gifts include gold coins. Children also receive special presents and sweet treats such as *aajil*, a mixture of nuts with raisins and other dried fruit.

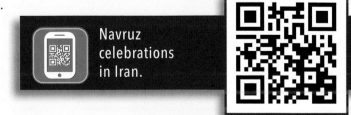

Navruz celebrations in Iran.

The first days of this 13-day observance are spent visiting older family members, as well as friends and other relatives. On the 13th day, everyone in Iran goes outdoors and heads to parks for a picnic. This day in nature is called *Seezdeh be dar* (which means "getting rid of the omen of the 13th day," or "to avoid bad luck on this day"). While picnicking, some Iranians also dance, listen to music, and take part in sporting events and other games. It is also customary for young women who hope to be married to go into a field and tie shoots from young plants into a knot, as a symbol of the marriage knot.

A CHANGE FOR THE HAFT SEEN TABLE

Wine was once a traditional part of Navruz, but it no longer is in Muslim countries where alcohol is prohibited. Wine has been replaced by vinegar on the Haft Seen table.

▲ An Iranian family celebrates at a festival for the Iranian new year, Navruz. The new solar year begins for Zoroastrians on the first day of spring, March 21.

■ Kosher for Passover in Israel

In Israel both secular and observant Jews celebrate Passover, and signs of the holiday appear throughout the country weeks ahead. It is easy to find Passover foods in the stores. Chocolate chips, cheese, and jams are labeled "Kosher for Passover" so that shoppers know that there are no forbidden ingredients. Even sugar, which often contains cornstarch, has a substitute corn-free kosher version. In addition to the stores, at the snack stands in public parks, kids are relieved to see that they can eat the ice cream, clearly marked "Kosher for Passover."

As Israel is a relatively new country, many people who live there still feel closely tied to the countries their families came from. The traditions of these many other countries shape Passover in Israel. For example, Jews from Iran pass around scallions during seder. While reciting a Passover song about God rescuing the Jews from Egypt, they lightly tap the scallions on the shoulder of the person on their right. This custom reminds Jews that their ancestors were slaves who were sometimes beaten.

Moroccan Jews living in Israel also have a special tradition, called Mimouna, that ends the seven days of Passover. In the days following the seder, Moroccan Jews make a variety of sweets–egg white cookies, coconut cakes with almond and chocolate, candied and dried fruits, jellies, and the almond paste marzipan. At the hour that Passover ends, Moroccan Jews set the Mimouna table and put out all the sweets. Then they place a fish–a fertility symbol–on a table outside their homes. Guests

▲ Ultra-Orthodox Jewish Hasidic children burn *chametz* (leavened bread foods) in the Mea Shearim neighborhood of Jerusalem prior to the start of the Passover holiday. Passover is a time when religious Jews thoroughly clean their homes and refrain from eating leavened bread.

arrive and sample the sweets and then move on to the next home where more Mimouna treats are offered.

More than 100,000 of the people living in Israel live in kibbutzim, communal farms whose residents work together to provide the community with food, clothing, a place to live, and medical services. A kibbutz seder might have a children's choir to sing the songs and many members to lead the seder. The kibbutz movement also created its own Haggadah–the Jewish collection of prayers and stories that tell the Exodus story–with some unique elements, including a special prayer to honor springtime.

THE GROWING KIBBUTZ MOVEMENT

The **kibbutz** was first established in the early 20th century, well before the Israeli State was formed. These communal farms grew the fruits and vegetables for which Israel is now well known. Today there are more than 250 kibbutzim in Israel and 100,000 members live there.

TEXT-DEPENDENT QUESTIONS

1: Who wrote the *Shahnameh*?

2: What are some foods consumed during the Moroccan Jewish tradition of Mimouna?

3: When was the kibbutz first established?

RESEARCH PROJECTS

1: Research information about the *Shahnameh*, including its content, characters, and relationship to Iranian history. Write a brief introduction to the poem based on your findings.

2: Research the history, traditions, and contemporary practices of the kibbutzim in Israel. Write a brief report that includes information about the state of the kibbutzim today and their role in Israeli society.

Celebrating in North America

Spring celebrations are popular across North America in March and April and include Easter, Passover, Holi, and Navruz. North America is a continent of immigrants from every corner of the world. The people of the United States and Canada pride themselves on the fact that their political history emphasizes freedom of expression and freedom of religion. At any given time during the springtime, there are celebrations and spring rites representing countless faiths and cultures. Still, North America is largely a Christian continent, and Easter, the holiday celebrating the Resurrection of Jesus Christ, is its most widespread spring celebration.

WORDS TO UNDERSTAND

Gender-neutral: Not specifying whether something is male or female.
Latticework: A pattern created with crossed strips of metal, wood, or other material.
Pogroms: Government-led campaigns of persecution.

◀ Revelers with colorful hats take part in the annual Easter Parade along Fifth Avenue in New York City.

Easter in North America

While the United States and Canada are not officially Christian, Good Friday in Canada is a national holiday, and in the United States the president recognizes Easter by sponsoring events such as the annual White House Egg Roll.

The focus on Christianity is not surprising given that it is practiced by close to 66 percent of all Canadians and 76 percent of Americans. Within the United States and Canada hundreds of Christian denominations exist, including many branches of Protestantism and Catholicism. Even people who do not practice any Christian faith may participate in some secular Easter traditions, such as dyeing eggs and eating chocolate.

Passover in North America

For Jewish communities throughout North America and the world, Passover commemorates the Exodus of the Jews from slavery in Egypt around 1200 B.C.E. The highlight of Passover is the observance of the seder at which the guests eat special kinds of food, listen to narratives about the Exodus from Egypt and freedom from slavery, sing songs, and offer special prayers.

Social change in North America has also affected this holiday tradition. As people in North America have grown more sensitive to the issue of equality between men and women, versions of the Haggadah have been developed that use **gender-neutral** words to describe God, and include mention of some of the important Jewish women throughout history. However, despite these changes, the Passover seder is easily recognizable whether one is in an Orthodox home or the home of Jews who follow a progressive approach to Judaism.

Growing Immigrant Groups Bring Their Spring Traditions

Spring festivals have been brought to North America by immigrants from all over the world. Latino Easter traditions such as Holy Week festivities are common in areas where there are immigrants from Latin America and the Caribbean, as well as in the southwest regions of the United States that were once part of Mexico. In communities such as New York City, where there are many Hindus, especially immigrants from India, Guyana, and Trinidad, Holi is celebrated in lavish style.

Find out about Holi celebrations in New York City.

▲ A boy fills his glass with grape juice in place of wine during a family Passover seder.

■ Easter in Canada

French explorers and colonists first brought Roman Catholicism to Canada. While the Protestant English eventually won control, Roman Catholicism has continued to dominate, especially in French-speaking areas of the country. Today the percentage of Roman Catholics in Canada is around 45 percent and only 23 percent identify themselves as Protestant. There are also approximately 400,000 Canadians who are members of the Eastern Orthodox Church.

In Canada, Good Friday is a national holiday. On this day, Christians may attend a special service mourning the death of Jesus. This service often lasts from noon until 3 P.M., representing the last three hours of darkness that Jesus suffered on the cross. Some Christians fast on this day. When they eat, it is generally fish instead of meat.

Today, there are approximately 1 million Canadians of Ukrainian descent. Canada and the Ukraine remain close friends, and Canada was the first country in the West to recognize the

▲ A priest blesses Easter baskets at a Ukrainian Catholic Church in Ontario, Canada.

Ukraine's independence from the Soviet Union in 1991. On Easter morning, Orthodox Ukrainians bring their Easter baskets to church to receive the priest's blessing. The baskets are heaped full of colored eggs, ham, beets with horseradish, Easter bread called *paska*, and cottage cheese. These foods are then eaten for Easter breakfast, beginning always with the colored eggs.

For the Ukrainians in Canada, eggs have another meaning. Craftspeople decorate eggs in an elaborate process called *pysanky* that is believed to transfer goodness from the household to the designs on the eggs, and thus to protect the family and home from misfortune. Spirals and other designs painted on the eggs are believed to trap evil, just as a spider traps a fly in the **latticework** of its web. Because of the meaning attached to the eggs, *pysanky* are distributed in a variety of ways: three or four might be placed on family graves, a couple go to the local priest, and in rural areas, several may be put under hens' nests to encourage good laying or under the beehive to ensure a plentiful production of honey.

As is true for Christians around the world, eggs, historically forbidden during Lent, are a treat during Easter. In parts of Quebec they are served with maple syrup, one of Canada's specialties. As in the United States, Canadian children also celebrate Easter with egg hunts in family yards and at local parks or church grounds. Because in Canada (and in northern parts of the United States) one cannot always count on having spring flowers and grass poking through the ground at Easter time, parents sometimes find themselves hiding chocolate and candy-filled eggs in snow banks.

■ Passover in Canada

Around 350,000 Jews live in Canada. Many Jews came to Canada in the 1880s to escape the **pogroms** (government-led campaigns of persecution) of eastern Europe and in the early 20th century to flee World War I and World War II and the Holocaust. Having fled religious oppression in their homelands, these Jews were often determined to express their faith and culture in Canada. Canada's Passover, then, reveals strong strains of Passover as it was celebrated in Europe.

Although Canada has a large Jewish population, kosher Passover foods are hard to come by in many Canadian stores. In cities with strong Jewish communities, such as Toronto and Montreal, kosher foods are available but expensive. And in smaller communities, they are not available at all. Canadian Jews have to be resourceful, checking labels carefully to avoid *chametz* (and, for Ashkenazi Jews, *kitniyot* as well) or preparing Passover foods from scratch.

■ Holi Can Be Frosty in Canada

More than 150,000 Canadians claim Hinduism as their religion. They or their ancestors come from all over the world—including East Africa, South Africa, Fiji, Mauritius, Guyana, Trinidad, India, Singapore, and Malaysia—and they often observe some of the traditions of their homelands.

Because it is often still quite cold in Canada when Holi comes, Hindus there tend

FUN WITHOUT FREEZING

A few determined Canadian Hindus refused to give up the water tradition of the holiday. In 2000 at York University in Ontario, a group of Hindu friends began an annual tradition of playing Holi outdoors regardless of the weather. In order to lessen the impact of being splashed with icy water on a cold Canadian day, they fill water bottles with hot water and stay close to sheltered areas of campus.

to celebrate indoors, often renting large halls for their gatherings. Some traditions must be adapted to the indoor setting. For example, Canadian Hindus still douse one another with colorful powder, but they leave out the water that would create a mess. Even so, they sometimes have to pay extra cleanup fees!

■ Persians of All Faiths Celebrate Navruz in Canada

More than 120,000 people of Iranian ancestry live in Canada, largely in urban areas, including Toronto, Vancouver, and Montreal. Recently the Canadian province of British Columbia officially recognized Navruz, or Norouz (as it is often spelled throughout the world). March 21 in British Columbia is now called Norouz, much to the delight of the thousands of Iranians who live there. All over Canada where Persians live, Navruz is celebrated in homes and community centers.

All Navruz celebrations include the traditional Haft Seen table, and many Persian celebrants wear traditional Iranian clothing and share dances with the many children. In order to attend some Navruz celebrations, families must purchase tickets. Other communities also have parades during Navruz and invite talented Persian musicians and dancers to participate.

■ The Spring Is Celebrated by Indigenous Canadians

The Inuit are the largest group of indigenous people in Canada. More than 55,000 Inuit live in the country's far north across 53 towns. In early April in the town of Iqualit the Inuit celebrate, and invite others to celebrate, Toonik Tyme. This spring festival began in 1964 as a way to unwind at the end of winter, as well as to attract tourism and to share Inuit traditions with non-Inuit people from Canada and beyond. The weeklong festival features events including seal hunting and skinning, harpoon throwing, igloo building, ice sculpture contests, dog team races, and a fishing derby (the first person to catch a fish wins). As is clear from the featured events, it may be spring in northern Canada, but it is usually still very cold, with temperatures averaging around 6 degrees Fahrenheit.

■ Easter in the United States

In the United States, Roman Catholics make up close to a quarter of all Christians, and Protestant denominations make up 52 percent. In addition, around 3 million people are members of Eastern

Orthodox churches. The Easter Bunny hopped its way into American Easter celebrations in the 18th century. The German custom of receiving a basket filled with candy by an Easter bunny came with European immigrants to Pennsylvania Dutch country, where it caught on. Children (good children anyway) woke on Easter to find colored eggs and other treats in a basket (the rabbit's nest). Today, the bunny still delivers. As in some parts of Europe, families in the United States paint Easter eggs together at home and participate in Easter egg hunts.

Many Protestants begin their celebration on Easter at a sunrise service in the United States. This tradition may have its roots in the Bible books of John, Matthew, and Luke, which suggest that Jesus' Resurrection happened before dawn. Ancient traditions might also have contributed to the ritual of the sunrise service, because many ancient cultures had spring rituals of building bonfires at dawn to symbolize the triumph of light and life over death and darkness. Whatever its true origins, the sunrise Easter service is one of great joy as the Sun comes up and overtakes the darkness of the night.

THE EASTER PARADE IN NEW YORK CITY

In many American churches, Easter is a time to wear one's finest clothing and hats. The women's fancy hats, or Easter "bonnets," are usually light-colored with a wide brim, decorated with ribbons, flowers, or other spring colors and themes. Easter hats gained even more popularity after the Irving Berlin song "Easter Parade" became famous in 1948. The song was featured in a film with the same title that starred two megastars of the time, Judy Garland and Fred Astaire.

From around the turn of the 19th century to the 20th, Americans often stretched their legs after church on Easter (and showed off their fine new clothes) by taking a walk around the town. These casual strolls may have eventually grown into the Easter parades that are now popular all over the United States. The grandest and most famous Easter Parade, the one that Berlin mentions in his celebrated song, is the annual parade in New York City along Fifth Avenue.

During the middle of the 19th century the upper class in New York City would parade in their new frocks and dress clothes after attending one of the Easter services at a Fifth Avenue church. Today, the parade is an extravaganza of outrageous outfits—from bonnets made of real flowers with live birds' nests in them, to high-fashion pets with their equally high-couture owners. Some simply choose to wear traditional Easter clothes. The parade is not highly organized and does not have floats or marching bands, but it is definitely the place to be in New York City on Easter Day.

EGG ROLLING ON THE WHITE HOUSE LAWN IN WASHINGTON, D.C.

Since President Rutherford B. Hayes's wife, Lucy, held the first public Easter egg roll on the lawn of the White House on Easter Monday in 1878, every Easter Monday, presidents and first ladies have welcomed the children onto the lawn. Children roll eggs across the lawn with spoons, not down a hill as is customary in Europe. Other activities include egg dyeing and decorating, and an egg hunt. Cabinet members and famous people such as musicians, movie stars, and the official White House Easter Bunny also come to spend time with the youngsters, some of them sharing their special talents. When the egg rolling is over, all participants leave with a special wooden egg that contains the signatures of the president and the first lady.

Today, to be admitted to the White House event, children must be between three and seven years old; they are issued free tickets on a first-come, first-served basis. In addition to the famous performers that attend every year, actors playing historical figures such as Lucy Hayes, Thomas Jefferson, Abraham Lincoln, and Betsy Ross wander the South Lawn entertaining the children. Some years the White House Easter egg collection is displayed. This collection is made up of eggs representing all 50 states and the District of Columbia, painted by talented local artists.

◼ Passover Traditions in the United States

The United States has the second-largest population of Jews in the world, at more than 5 million. The number of Jews in the United States is just slightly smaller than in Israel today. Especially in large cities where an overwhelming majority of U.S. Jews live, strong support systems exist to help Jews carry on their Passover traditions. Indeed, even among nonreligious Jews in the United States, Passover is widely celebrated as a way of passing cultural traditions on to the next generation. In the United States, Jews often invite non-Jewish friends to the Passover table to share in the celebration.

On college campuses close to Jewish communities, it is often possible to attend an Orthodox Hasidic Passover at Chabad Houses, which, according to the Chabad House of Greater Boston, are "dedicated to furthering the understanding and observance of Jewish traditions to all, regardless of their background." These houses provide a "home away from home" for Jewish students and young adults who live far from their families, as well as others within the communities. Hasidic rabbis live in or work with the houses, which can be found in Boston, Massachusetts; Los Angeles, California; Ann Arbor, Michigan; Amherst, Massachusetts; Hartford, Connecticut; Boca Raton, Florida, and many other communities.

Since Passover is a ritual feast, the same basic steps are followed at seders in New York, Chicago, or Los Angeles as in Jerusalem. But although the outline of the seder remains consistent across time and national borders, Jews are free to drop parts of the ceremony or add elements from other faiths (such as African-American spirituals or modern poetry) that make connections between the Israelites' bondage and the enslavement of other peoples.

▲ Young Indian-Americans join in a mud sliding activity as part of the Holi festival of colors at a college in South Carolina

Holi Parades and Parties across the United States

Approximately 1 million Hindus of Indian and Indo-Caribbean descent live in the United States, most in major urban centers on the East and West coasts. In New York City, Indians of Trinidadian and Guyanese descent celebrate the Caribbean version of Holi. The tradition began in 1990 in Queens with a large public parade including floats carrying beauty queen contest winners, prominent business people, politicians, and religious leaders. In a restriction unheard of in India, the colorful Holi dyes are not allowed along the parade route. Celebrants must hold their fire until they get to a community park at the end of the parade. There, children and adults alike douse one another with water and colored powder, or *abrac*. Even innocent bystanders are fair targets for kids firing super-soakers filled with purple dye.

Persians of all Faiths Celebrate Navruz throughout the United States

Persians around the country celebrate Navruz by organizing fire jumps, parades, and parties. In New York City, a large parade features traditional Iranian dancing and elaborate floats. At universities around the country, Persian and Iranian students organize Navruz events. In Persian homes, as well as the homes of the Baha'is, the Haft Seen table will be prepared with the traditional objects, and might also include the holy books of many faiths—the Quran, Christian Bible, or writings of the Baha'i prophet Bahaullah.

On the West Coast, where many Iranians live, the Navruz New Year's countdown is shown on TV. Community centers play host to Iranians as well as non-Persian friends and neighbors who are along for the party. These community centers are important to the lives of Persians throughout the year, not just at Navruz. They also offer Farsi language classes and other cultural activities for children and adults and many welcome people of all backgrounds to participate in their unique and diverse culture.

TEXT-DEPENDENT QUESTIONS

1: Who brought Roman Catholicism to Canada?

2: What indigenous population celebrates Toonik Tyme?

3: What is a "Chabad House"?

RESEARCH PROJECTS

1: Research the history, sacred writings, and important figures of the Baha'i Faith. Write a brief overview of the faith with special attention to its place in the world today and the beliefs of contemporary Baha'is.

2: Research one of the indigenous communities of Canada, such as the Inuit, First Nations, or Métis peoples. Find out about their history, culture, language, religious beliefs, and other details. Write a brief overview summarizing your findings.

▲ Greek Orthodox Canadians attend a midnight Service of the Resurrection in Winnipeg. The priest and parishioners are holding white candles lit with the holy flame.

Celebrating in Oceania

Oceania is an area in the Pacific Ocean that cradles the **equator**. Consisting of thousands of islands, the area is usually divided into three main regions: Polynesia, Micronesia, and Melanesia. The countries of Oceania include Australia, New Zealand, the Marshall Islands, Federated States of Micronesia, Papua New Guinea, Samoa, and Tonga. Almost all of Oceania is located in the Southern Hemisphere, which means that

WORDS TO UNDERSTAND

Bilby: A small marsupial native to Australia, with a long nose and long ears.

Drought: A prolonged period without rain.

Equator: The imaginary line that extends around the Earth and that divides it into two halves. Each half is equal in distance from the north and south poles. The equator goes through the northern part of South America and central Africa.

Legacy: Something that is passed down from a generation before. It can be something material such as an inheritance or a tradition or custom that is handed down through the generations.

◄ In Australia traditional chocolate Easter bunnies have been joined by chocolate Easter bilbies, like the one shown here. Bilbies, also known as rabbit-eared bandicoots, are an endangered species in Australia.

most "spring" celebrations of Easter and Holi actually happen in the Oceanian fall, when the weather is usually warm and dry (the coldest months are in June, July, and August).

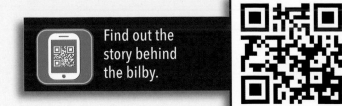

Find out the story behind the bilby.

In the 1800s Britain colonized many parts of Oceania, including New Zealand, Australia, parts of Micronesia, and Fiji, introducing Christianity to the indigenous people. By the 1970s Britain no longer held colonial power in this area, but many of the people still practiced Christianity. In Fiji, where the British had imported workers from India, a Hindu **legacy** remains. Today, more than 65 percent of Australians and more than 50 percent of New Zealanders practice some form of Christianity. In Fiji 50 percent are Christian and around 30 percent practice Hinduism.

THE SENSITIVE BILBY

Bilbies are also known as rabbit-eared bandicoots and are mostly found in the driest regions of interior Australia. With big ears, long hind legs, and bushy tails, the bilby can smell and hear very well, but has poor eyesight. For this reason, and because temperatures are cooler after sunset, bilbies mostly come out at night to eat. Their diet includes small insects such as termites and ants, seeds, fungi, and roots that they rake out of the sandy desert soil with their sharp claws and long tongues. The bilbies used to thrive in Australia but their population has dwindled. They must compete with rabbits for food, and foxes and feral cats hunt them. **Droughts** have killed some bilbies, as has poison meant to control the huge overpopulation of wild rabbits. Some of the land where bilbies used to live is now reserved for cattle and other livestock.

■ Buns and Easter Bilbies in Australia

Easter is observed in Australia primarily by people of Anglo-Irish origin. They attend church services early in the morning and later have hot cross buns for breakfast. Children receive chocolate eggs or eggs made of sugar that contain little toys. On Easter Sunday many families gather for a holiday meal, often roast lamb, beef, or chicken with roasted vegetables such as potatoes, carrots, and pumpkin, followed by an Easter egg hunt. In Australia, the traditional chocolate Easter bunny has been joined by a chocolate Easter **bilby**, an animal native to Australia

▲ Easter weekend heralds the International Kite Festival in Adelaide, Australia, which attracts thousands of kite flyers from around the world.

that is now an endangered species. Chocolate manufacturers contribute some of their bilby profits toward protecting the animal from extinction.

■ Easter Celebrations in Fiji

In Fiji, Good Friday is a day to mourn in church. During a somber service, Christians meditate on Jesus' suffering and death on the cross. On some islands Christians take part in Good Friday processions and reenactments of the Crucifixion. The main service on Good Friday takes place between midday and 3 P.M. In many churches, it takes the form of a meditation based on the few last words of Jesus on the cross, with hymns, prayers, and short sermons.

On Easter in Fiji the churches are decorated with flowers, and people sing hymns and special songs. The Monday after Easter is a national holiday with government offices, businesses, and schools closed for the day.

■ Easter Begins on Saturday in New Zealand

In New Zealand, Easter ceremonies begin on the night of Holy Saturday with an evening service. At church on Easter Sunday worshippers light large candles symbolizing hope and pass them from hand to hand. People also enjoy a special cake on Easter called *sinnel*, prepared with dried fruit and whisky or brandy. Because the Easter holiday lasts from Good Friday through the following Tuesday, New Zealanders often travel, spending Easter at their family homes or farms in the countryside.

■ Easter Is Both Sacred and Fun in Tonga

In Tonga, where the people are devout Christians, the festival of Easter assumes great importance. Apart from the traditional ceremonial prayers in churches, the people also organize a grand festival, complete with youth choirs, passion plays, concerts, and other cultural performances. Easter Monday is a public holiday, and Tongans take advantage of the long weekend to enjoy themselves with friends and family.

TEXT-DEPENDENT QUESTIONS

1: What are the three main regions of Oceania?

2: Where are chocolate bilbies eaten during Easter?

3: What special ingredients are used in preparing *sinnel*?

RESEARCH PROJECTS

1: Research one of the major islands of Oceania, including facts about its size, geography, notable features, and other information. Write a brief overview of the island that summarizes your findings.

2: Research the Jewish population in Australia, including main population centers, history, and contributions to Australian culture. Write a brief report that summarizes your findings, touching on any special Australian Passover traditions.

Series Glossary

ancestors The direct family members of one who is deceased

aristocrat A member of a high social class, the nobility, or the ruling class

atonement The act of making up for sins so that they may be forgiven

ayatollah A major religious leader, scholar, and teacher in Shii Islam; the religious leader of Iran

colonial era A period of time between the 17th to 19th century when many countries of the Americas and Africa were colonized by Europeans.

colonize To travel to and settle in a foreign land that has already been settled by groups of people. To colonize can mean to take control of the indigenous groups already in the area or to wield power over them in order to control their human and physical resources.

commemorate To honor the memory of a person or event

commercialization The act of reorganizing or reworking something in order to extract profit from it

descendant One who comes from a specific ancestor

Eastern Orthodox Church The group of Christian churches that includes the Greek Orthodox, Russian Orthodox, and several other churches led by patriarchs in Istanbul (Constantinople), Jerusalem, Antioch, and Alexandria.

effigy A representation of someone or something, often used for mockery

equinox Either of the two times during each year when night and day are approximately the same length of time. The spring equinox typically falls around March 21 and the autumnal equinox around September 23.

fast To abstain from eating for a set period of time, or to eat at only prescribed times of the day as directed by religious custom or law.

feast day A day when a religious celebration occurs and an intricate feast is prepared and eaten.

firsthand From the original source; experienced in person

Five Pillars of Islam The five duties Muslims must observe: declaring that there is only one God and Muhammad is his prophet, praying five times a day, giving to charity, fasting during Ramadan, and making a pilgrimage to Mecca

foundation myth A story that describes the foundation of a nation in a way that inspires its people

Gregorian calendar The calendar in use through most of the world

hedonism The belief that pleasure is the sole good in life

Hindu A follower of Hinduism, the dominant religion of India

imam A leader; a scholar of Islam; the head of a mosque

indigenous Originating in or native to a specific region; often refers to living things such as people, animals, and plants

Islam The religious faith of Muslims. Muslims believe that Allah is the only God, and Muhammad was his prophet

Judaism A religion that developed among the ancient Hebrews. Followers of Judaism believe in one God and follow specific laws written in the Torah and the Talmud, and revealed to them by Moses.

Julian calendar Is named after Julius Caesar, a military leader and dictator of ancient Rome, who introduced it in 46 B.C.E. The Julian calendar has 365 days divided into 12 months, and begins on January 1. An extra day, or leap day, is added every four years (February 29) so that the years will average out to 365.242, which is quite close to the actual 365.242199 days of Earth's orbit.

lower realm In the Asian tradition, the place where the souls end up if their actions on Earth were not good

lunar Related to the Moon

martyr A person who willingly undergoes pain or death because of a strong belief or principle

masquerade A party to which people wear masks, and sometimes costumes or disguises

millennium 1,000 years

monarch A king or queen; a ruler who inherits the throne from a parent or other relative

monotheism The belief in the supremacy of one god (and not many) that began with Judaism more than 4,000 years ago and also includes the major religions of Islam and Christianity.

mosque An Islamic house of worship

mourning The expression of sorrow for the loss of a loved one, typically involving

movable feast A religious feast day that occurs on a different day every year

Muhammad The prophet to whom God revealed the Quran, considered the final prophet of Islam

mullah A clergyman who is an expert on the Quran and Islamic religious matters

Muslim A person who follows the Islamic religion

New Testament The books of the Bible that were written after the birth of Christ

New World A term used to describe the Americas from the point of view of the Western Europeans (especially those from France, England, Portugal, and Spain) who colonized and settled what is today North and South America.

offering Donation of food or money given in the name of a deity or God

Old Testament The Christian term for the Hebrew Scriptures of the Bible, written before the birth of Christ

oral tradition Stories told aloud, rather than written, as a way to pass down history

pagan Originally, someone in ancient Europe who lived in the countryside; a person or group that does not believe in one god, but often believes in many gods that are closely connected to nature and the natural world

pageantry Spectacle, elaborate display

parody Imitation of something, exaggerated for comic effect—for example, a parody of science fiction movies.

patria Fatherland; nation; homeland

peasant People who farm land that usually belongs to someone else, such as a landowner

penance The repentance of sins, including confessing, expressing regret for having committed them, and doing something to earn forgiveness

piety A strong belief in and correspondingly fervent practice of religion

pilgrimage A journey undertaken to a specific destination, often for religious purposes

prank A mischievous or humorous trick

pre-Columbian Of or relating to the period before Christopher Columbus arrived in the Americas

procession A group of people moving together in the same direction, especially in a type of celebration

prophecy A prediction about a future event

prophet An individual who acts as the interpreter or conveyer of the will of God and spreads the word to the followers or possible followers of a religion. A prophet can also be a stirring leader or teacher of a religious group. Capitalized it refers to Muhammad.

Protestant A member of a Christian denomination that does not follow the rule of the pope in Rome and is not one of the Eastern Orthodox Churches. Protestant denominations include Anglicans (Episcopalians), Lutherans, Presbyterians, Methodists, Baptists, and many others.

Quran The holy book of Islam

rabbi A Jew who is ordained to lead a Jewish congregation; rabbis are traditionally teachers of Judaism.

reincarnation The belief in some religions that after a person or animal dies, his or her soul will be reborn in another person or animal; it literally means, "to be made flesh again." Many Indian religions such as Hinduism, Sikhism, and Jainism, believe in reincarnation.

repentance To express regret and ask forgiveness for doing something wrong or hurtful.

requiem A Mass for the souls of the dead, especially in the Catholic Church

revel To celebrate in a joyful manner; to take extreme pleasure

ritual A specific action or ceremony typically of religious significance

sacred Connected with God or religious purposes and deemed worthy of veneration and worship

sacrifice Something given up or offered in the name of God, a deity or an ancestor.

shaman A spiritual guide who a community believes has unique powers to tell the future and to heal the sick. Shamans can mediate or cooperate with spirits for a community's advantage. Cultures that practice shamanism are found all over the world still today.

Shia A Muslim sect that believes that Ali, Muhammad's son-in-law, should have succeeded Muhammad as the caliph of Islam; a common sect in Iran but worldwide encompassing only about 15 percent of Muslims

solar calendar A calendar that is based on the time it takes Earth to orbit once around the Sun

solar Related to the Sun

solilunar Relating to both the Sun and Moon

solstice Day of the year when the hours of daylight are longest or shortest. The solstices mark the changing of the seasons–when summer begins in the Northern Hemisphere (about June 22) and winter begins in the Northern Hemisphere (about December 22).

spiritual Of or relating to the human spirit or soul, or to religious belief

Sunni The largest Islamic sect, including about 85 percent of the world's Muslims

supernatural Existing outside the natural world

Talmud The document that encompasses the body of Jewish law and customs

Torah Jewish scriptures, the first five books of the Hebrew scriptures, which serve as the core of Jewish belief

veneration Honoring a god or a saint with specific practices

vigil A period in which a person stays awake to await some event

Vodou A religion rooted in traditional African beliefs that is practiced mostly in Haiti, although it is very popular in the West Indies as well. Outside of Haiti it is called *Vodun*.

Further Resources

■ Books

12 Major World Religions: The Beliefs, Rituals, and Traditions of Humanity's Most Influential Faiths. By Jason Boyett. Published in 2016 by Zephyros Press, Berkeley, Calif. A sound introduction to the world's major religions, including Christianity, Judaism, and Islam.

Hinduism: A Very Short Introduction, 2nd Ed. By Kim Knott. Published in 2016 by Oxford University Press, Oxford, UK. The revised edition of this compact yet thorough survey of Hinduism provides new information on the impact of technology and social media on Hindus, political developments in India, and other issues.

Passover: Festival of Freedom. By Monqiue Polak. Published in 2016 by Orca Book Publishers, Victoria, British Columbia. A unique, personal account of the Passover story, from its ancient origins to its contemporary significance.

Rick Steves' European Easter. By Rick Steves. Published in 2016 by Rick Steves/Avalon Travel, Berkeley, Calif. Join beloved tour guide and television personality Rick Steves on a journey through Europe's most fascinating Easter traditions, from blessings of olive branches in Tuscany, Italy, to elaborate floats in Sevilla, Spain.

Judaism (Major World Religions). By Adam Lewinsky. Published in 2017 by Mason Crest, Broomall, Pa. This volume is one in a series exploring the world's major religious traditions. It explores the history, beliefs, and practices of Judaism from ancient times through the present.

Holi (World's Greatest Celebrations). By Michelle Lee. Published in 2016 by Scobre Educational, La Jolla, Calif. An overview of the festival of Holi, including its history, traditions, and centers of celebration.

■ Web Sites

Festival of Colors in India. http://www.thecolorsofindia.com/holi.html. A lively and informative set of pages on Holi history and celebration, this forms part of the much larger Colors of India cultural Web site.

History.com. http://www.history.com/topics/holidays/history-of-easter. A Web site with interactive material and photos about the history and celebrations of Easter.

Iranian Chamber Society. http://www.iranchamber.com/culture/articles/norooz_iranian_new_year.php. Web site that clearly and succinctly explains many aspects of this fascinating ancient observance. Also includes a selection of traditional Navruz greetings.

The Jewish Virtual Library. http://www.jewishvirtuallibrary.org/passover-pesach. This online encyclopedia provides extensive and easy-to-follow explanations of practically every aspect of Judaism. Here, one can better understand all Jewish celebrations, as well as the history of Judaism, important Jewish women, the Holocaust, biographies of famous Jews in every field imaginable, and vital information on Israel.

ThoughtCo: Judaism. https://www.thoughtco.com/all-about-passover-pesach-2076435. Good Web site with information and images related to Passover.

Index

ancestor worship 43, 49
Ascension Day 63–64

bilbies 104
Bituun 59

camel races 45–46
Carnival 14
Choti Holi (Small Holi) 38
Coptic Easter 46–47

Eostre 12, 17
Exodus 20–22, 77, 89, 92

fast 15, 46–47, 93
feast day 12, 28
festival of colors. *See* Holi
Firing of the Judases 82
four questions 22

Good Friday 13, 16, 46, 72, 92–93, 105–106

Haft Seen 31–32, 54–55, 86–87, 96, 100
Hanuman 40
Holi 8, 35–40, 47–49, 53–54, 57, 59, 64, 76,
    78–79, 91–92, 95, 100, 104, 106
Holika 36, 40, 54, 57, 59

Israelite 19–22, 24

Kosher for Passover 88, 95
Krishna 37, 40, 57

Lent 6, 14–15 95

Mardi Gras (Fat Tuesday) 14
Maundy Thursday 46
Moon 12–14, 35, 58, 78
Moses 19–21
Mwaka Kogwa. *See* Navruz 49–50

Navruz *See also* Mwaka Kogwa 8, 27–32,
    45, 49–50, 53–58, 60–61, 85–87, 91,
    96, 100

passion play 75, 77, 82, 106
Passover seder 22–23, 92
Prahlada 36, 40

Resurrection 7, 11, 13, 16, 46, 60, 63–64,
    70–72, 78–79, 91, 97

Sprinkling Day 69

Toonik Tyme 96
Tsagaan Tsar 58–59

Vappu 66
Vishnu 36–37, 40

Picture Credits